believe beyond

DISCOVER THE POWER OF UNWAVERING BELIEF

May 9. 2025

Dear Andrea + Victoria – both of you bring a fresh spring energy with you in your aura every time you arrive!

Blessings,
E Hitchcott Scott

believe beyond

DISCOVER THE POWER OF
UNWAVERING BELIEF

www.katebutlerbooks.com

The author, publisher, and contributors shall not be liable for any misuse of the enclosed material. This book is strictly for informational and educational purposes only. The author, publisher, and contributors do not guarantee that anyone following these techniques, suggestions, tips, ideas, or strategies will heal or become successful. The author, publisher, and contributors shall have neither liability nor responsibility to anyone with respect to any loss or damage caused, or alleged to be caused, directly or indirectly, by the information or suggestions contained in this book.

To the extent that any business, investment, or financial strategies are shared, they are shared for informational and educational purposes only. This book does not guarantee results or provide legal, tax, investment, or financial advice. Consult your legal, tax, investment, or financial professional.

To the extent that any medical or health information is shared in this book, it is shared as an information and education resource only and is not to be used or relied on for any diagnostic or treatment purposes. Any such information is not intended to be patient information, does not create any patient-physician relationship, and should not be used as a substitute for professional diagnosis and treatment. Neither the author, publisher, nor contributors provide health or healing advice. Consult your healthcare professional.

ISBN: 978-1-962407-72-4 (paperback)
ISBN: 978-1-962407-71-7 (hardcover)
ISBN: 978-1-962407-73-1 (eBook)

Design by Melissa Williams Design
mwbookdesign.com

This book is dedicated to you. We see you, we feel you, we relate to you, and we connect with you . . . because we are you. At our core, we are more alike than we are different. We are beings of light and love who deeply desire to make a positive influence on the world with our unique type of brilliance. The pages of this book promise to fill you with the wisdom, insights, and inspiration that will align you further with your soul's path. Our hope is that the vulnerability and authenticity of these pages will remind you deeply of who you are and inspire you to claim your dreams, shine your light, and step into the legacy you are meant to leave in this world.

It is your time. It is our time. It is time.

Enjoy the unfolding . . .

table of contents

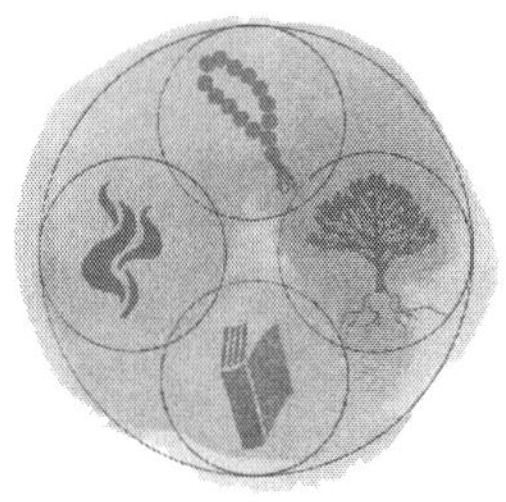

INTRODUCTION

KATE BUTLER, INSPIRED IMPACT SERIES CREATOR

Life is a magnificent journey of limitless possibilities, shaped by the beliefs we hold and the courage to step beyond what we once thought possible. Every experience—big or small—plays a vital role in our personal growth and the unfolding of our unique purpose. In this book, we will explore the profound power of choosing to **Believe Beyond**—beyond doubts, beyond fear, beyond perceived limitations. Together, we will discover how embracing this mindset can unlock infinite opportunities and extraordinary transformation.

Life unfolds moment by moment, urging us to evolve, explore, and reach beyond where we feel comfortable. To believe beyond means to trust that we are never truly finished growing, that our story is still being written, and that our greatest breakthroughs are yet to come . . . if we allow them in! When we embrace this truth, we open the door to limitless potential in every area of our lives.

Life's journey is a balance between discovery and becoming.. As we take steps forward, we encounter challenges, successes, awakenings, and moments of profound insight. Each experience helps to shape us along the way. When we believe beyond what we think we can handle, we step into a life that is more expansive and more aligned with our true purpose.

Let's talk about the magic! As we believe beyond, there are going to be moments of magic along the way. It is essential to pause and embrace these times in our lives when the magic is unfolding! Our purpose isn't found in reaching a final destination but in believing beyond what we see in the present moment. Each step we take—each lesson, each challenge, each success—propels us toward our highest potential. By embracing the unknown and trusting the journey, we allow new opportunities to unfold in ways we never imagined. When we shift from needing certainty to embracing possibility, we unlock the power of believing beyond our current reality. And . . . this . . . is truly when life gets delightful!

Shifting our perspective allows us to see challenges not as roadblocks, but as stepping-stones to something greater. It invites us to release fear, let go of external expectations, and instead trust the unfolding of our path. When we believe beyond the limits we once placed on ourselves, we experience expansion, new opportunities, and a life that exceeds our wildest dreams. I am available for that. Are you?

The power of presence fuels our ability to believe beyond. To fully embrace each moment, we must cultivate a deep sense of mindful awareness. By grounding ourselves in the present, we begin to see past limitations and recognize the possibilities waiting for us instead. Practicing mindfulness isn't just about being present; it's about being open. It's about believing beyond what seems possible and allowing ourselves to fully experience the beauty, depth, and richness of each moment. The small details—a sweet word, a sparkling sunrise, a moment of clarity or an a-ha moment—become powerful reminders that life is happening for us, and that the next opening is on its way . . . because it always is.

Shifting our perspective allows us to see challenges not as roadblocks, but as stepping-stones to something greater. It invites us to release fear, let go of external expectations, and instead trust the unfolding of our path. When we believe beyond the limits we once placed on ourselves, we experience expansion, new opportunities, and a life that exceeds our wildest dreams. I am available for that. Are you?

Believing Beyond can show up in our lives in all ways, always. Imagine living choosing to also believe beyond what seems ordinary. Imagine finding purpose in the small, everyday choices, in the way we show up, the love we share and the way we share it, in the connections we make and in the simple words we speak. I believe when we find purpose in the ordinary this is the moment life actually becomes extraordinary. And this is available to each and every one of us in all ways, always.

The ripple effect of believing beyond is immeasurable. When we choose to embrace life fullt we create a ripple effect that touches everyone around us. By believing beyond our fears and doubts, we inspire others to do the same.

Our impact extends far beyond what we can see. A kind word, a moment of encouragement, a reminder that "anything is possible" can alter the course of someone's life. By believing beyond for ourselves, we pave the way for others to rise alongside us. Growth is a collective experience, where our expansion contributes to the transformation of those around us, as well. How beautiful is this?

So we invite you . . . to unlock a life beyond your wildest imagination and to . . . Believe Beyond.

With a
Grateful Heart
– Kate ♡

ABOUT KATE BUTLER, CPSC

Kate Butler is a Certified Professional Success Coach and the founder of Inspired Impact Publishing where she has published over 650 #1 Best-selling Authors under the inspirational umbrella. Kate's most recent #1 International Best-seller is the Daily Inspirational Quote and Prompt Book, "All Things Are Possible"!

Kate recently decided to test her own motto of "All Things Being Possible" when she packed up her family to move to Europe for 3 months to work, explore, travel and learn. Kate and her daughters ended up on an International Book Tour to Ireland, UK and Italy for three months sharing their books with children across the globe. Kate truly, truly believes, if she can fulfill her dreams, anyone can, and she is committed to being your biggest cheerleader along the way.

Kate offers clients dynamic programs to help her clients reach their ultimate potential and live out their dreams. She does this through book publishing programs, speaking and media programs and mindset programs. Kate is also the creator of the Inspired Impact Book Series, which provides clients an opportunity to share their story in a book and become a published author in a book collective!

Kate received her double major degree in Mass Communications and Interpersonal Communication Studies from Towson University in Maryland. After ten years in the corporate world, Kate decided it was time to fulfill her true passion; she studied business at Wharton School of Business at The University of Pennsylvania and received her certificate in Entrepreneur Acceleration.

Throughout Kate's journey in the thought leader space, she has been featured alongside Jack Canfield, creator of Chicken Soup for the Soul, when they were both featured in an Emmy Nominated documentary, "Deep Talk With The Masters". This led to her own TV Show, "Where All Things Are Possible" which she loves hosting to bring hope and healing to millions on a weekly basis. Kate has also written books with Les Brown, Lisa Nichols, and Iyanla Vanzant to name a few. Kate's expertise has been featured on Fox 29, GoodDay Philadelphia, HBO, PHL 17, PBS and Sesame Street. However she is most proud of her feature in the Huffington Post where they officially coined her "The Real Deal of the Coaching Industry."

To learn more about becoming an author in the Inspired Impact Book Series, or to learn how to work with Kate directly on achieving your goals or publishing your book (including children's books), visit her website at www.katebutlerbooks.com. Kate would love to connect with you!

To connect with Kate

Facebook: @katebutlerbooks
Instagram: @katebutlerbooks
Website: www.katebutlerbooks.com

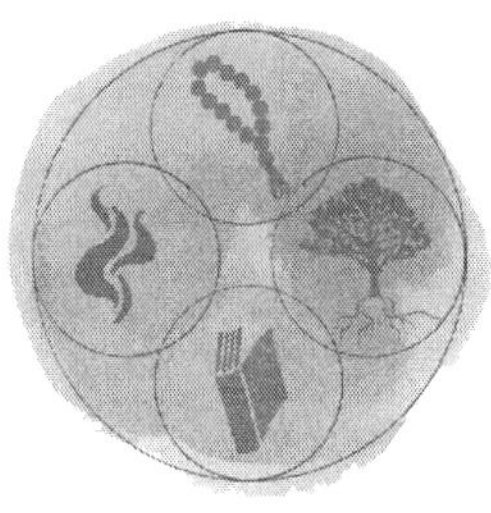

FOREWORD

Patty Aubery

Life has a way of surprising us, doesn't it? It can lift us to exhilarating heights, cradle us in moments of bliss, and yet, in an instant, it can snatch it all away, leaving us grappling with a sense of profound loss. These are the moments that shake us to our core, revealing the fragile nature of our existence and reminding us of the urgency to embrace every precious second we have.

I still remember the day when my world tilted on its axis. It was a time of darkness, a time when my heart became heavy with grief and my spirit yearned for solace. My mother, my pillar of strength, had been diagnosed with breast cancer, a relentless adversary that threatened to steal her away from us. As her body weakened, her spirit grew stronger, and she taught me one of the most valuable lessons life has ever bestowed upon me.

In the quiet moments we shared, she looked into my eyes, her voice filled with love and determination. "Promise me," she whispered, "promise me that you will not hide. Embrace life in all its rawness, in all its vulnerability. Promise me that you will seize every moment, for it is in those moments that life's true magic resides."

Those words pierced my heart, etching themselves deep into my being. They became my compass, guiding me through the labyrinth of grief, and inspiring me to make the most of the time I have been granted. It is this personal journey, forged through loss and fueled by an unwavering love, that led me to share my story within the pages of this book.

As you embark on this reading journey, I invite you to connect with the universal truths that bind us all together. Life's moments—both the magnificent and the devastating—have a way of shaping us, transforming us into the individuals we are meant to become. In the midst of heartache, we discover our resilience, our capacity for compassion, and our unwavering spirit. And in the moments of pure joy, we uncover the essence of what it means to truly live.

This book is not just about my story; it is about our shared humanity. It is an invitation to reflect upon your own journey, the pivotal moments that have marked your path, and the legacy you are creating through the choices you make. It is a reminder that life's fragility is a gift—an urgent call to embrace the fleeting nature of our existence, to hold close those we cherish, and to honor the moments that touch our souls.

As you read these pages, allow yourself to be fully present. Let the stories shared here stir something within you, perhaps awakening dormant dreams or reminding you of the value of the relationships that enrich your life. May you find solace, inspiration, and a renewed commitment to live authentically, cherishing each moment as the precious gift that it is.

In life, even in the difficult moments, we have a choice—to retreat and hide from life's uncertainties, or to step boldly into the world, allowing our hearts to remain open to all that it offers. It is my deepest desire that this book serves as a gentle reminder to seize every opportunity, to celebrate the beauty of each fleeting moment, and to embrace the fragility of life with courage and grace.

Dear reader, as you embark on this profound exploration of life's fleeting moments, I extend my hand to you, knowing that within the pages of this book, we share a common thread of resilience, loss, and the unwavering pursuit of meaning. Together, let us walk this path, honoring the memories that have shaped us and the moments that continue to shape us still. In our shared experiences, may we find solace, connection, and the inspiration to embrace life with unwavering courage and an unyielding appreciation for the precious moments that make up our existence.

With heartfelt gratitude,

Patty Aubery

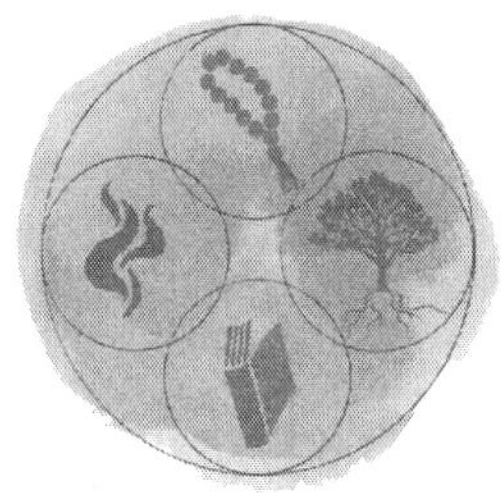

SUDDENLY ALONE & RISING STRONGER

Raida Abdulsalam Abu-Issa

Have you lost your way home? Fear not—I did too. Yet, in the most unexpected moments, life has a mysterious way of guiding you back to where you truly belong.

My True Essence

I grew up in a business-minded family and seeing the good in everything and communicating with love is ingrained in my DNA.

My passion for learning and expanding my knowledge in child psychology and self-development has given me a deeper understanding of my emotions and triggers, as well as the right tools to explore new possibilities for growth and transformation. I'm like a kaleidoscope—I can't live in boxes and limitations.

Train of Life

The journey of life is a tapestry woven from joyous beginnings, instilling values, and profound losses, each thread revealing the complexity of the journey.

My story begins in the playful embrace of early childhood in Qatar and the Emirates, where laughter painted my days with innocent joy. As I transitioned to Lebanon, I found serenity and a deep bond with my father, whose love nurtured my sensitive spirit and fueled my dreams of dancing through life. Growing up, we were surrounded by diversity and a wide range of experiences that instilled in us resilience and adaptability for the future.

Facing the Unexpected

The comfort of childhood gave way to the turbulence of adolescence. From the ages of 10 to 21, I faced the challenge of adaptation, learning to navigate a world that often misjudged my intentions and sensitivity as we moved to London unexpectedly. Amidst strict rules and the weight of comparison, I found solace in my family connections, wrestling with the complexities of responsibility and the pain of feeling misunderstood.

The defining moment came when I was 18. The loss of my father shook the very foundation of my existence, propelling me into a journey of self-discovery that took me from London to Paris. It was a path marked by grief and solitude yet illuminated by the unexpected closeness I found with my soulmate, who became a beacon of support in my darkest hours. Through this intricate dance of joy, pain, and resilience, I learned that even the softest hearts can forge paths of strength and purpose.

Building Family and Career

My career path began with working in our family business, which evolved into investing in various industries, harnessing my natural entrepreneurial spirit. This ultimately led me to become an artist and a growth mindset coach, driven by my passion for teaching others how to channel their emotions and discover effective coping mechanisms rather than being dependent on antidepressants.

I married the love of my life, and together we established our shared values, boundaries, responsibilities, and priorities. While we've faced our fair share of ups and downs, challenges, and obstacles, we've strengthened our relationship through open communication, respect, and a deep commitment to growing together.

Together, we raised five grown children, and it took significant effort to balance a full-time career while staying deeply involved in their education, ensuring they didn't encounter difficulties along the way. Managing both family and work was challenging, but I remained dedicated to helping them thrive. My mother often told me, "You can't have both. It's either family or career." Yet, with the right support, I found that anything is possible. I acknowledge my husband, who believed in my leadership skills, and his continuous support.

It was never on our radar to be separated as a couple. The idea felt distant, almost unthinkable. Yet here we were, navigating a decision shaped by necessity. In 2014, we made the tough choice that I would move to Austria for three years with our three younger children. The changes in the education system loomed large, and it would impact them later in life. Did you know that moving from one country to another has the same impact as the loss of a loved one?

Showing Up in the Name of Love

Fast forward, my husband got diagnosed with stage 4 colon cancer. It was traumatizing news. Being in Austria and having residency gave us the opportunity to have different choices for his treatment plan. The journey lasted for three years, not forgetting the restrictions of travel as it was during COVID-19. Faced with doubts from our surroundings about his treatment plan, the way we dealt with him was unbearable even though I was following the doctors' instructions.

I immersed myself in learning about the psychological and medical challenges and side effects of chemo that come with battling cancer. There were times I just wanted to disappear off the face of the earth and come back when he was healed.

Besides, my surroundings discounted my unexpressed emotions of seeing my partner, husband, and friend getting weaker and weaker by the day and suffering, yet I had to be brave and smile. Being on alert, fearing to get the sudden news—He's gone!

The Weight of Losses

Picture the scene: my mother had just passed away, yet I didn't shed a tear. My husband had broken down in front of me, and I found myself caught in an overwhelming emotional roller coaster. I held my grief silently, shattered into invisible pieces. The heartbreak I should have felt for my mother was swallowed whole, tucked away in the deepest corners of my soul. She was gone, but I had to stay strong for him, as we were alone together in Austria. In those moments, I couldn't afford to lend an ear to any outside noise or distractions; I had to remain focused on supporting myself and my loved ones.

In the final three months of his life, we found ourselves in Qatar. He had asked for the therapist to come, but it soon became clear that the support was truly for me. Two weeks before he passed, in a quiet moment at the hospital, he turned to me and asked, "Where do you want me to be?" At first, I didn't understand. Then, with a wave of realization, I replied, "Wherever you want." He paused, looked at me gently, and said, "Whichever is easier for you." I answered, "All is possible." Despite the unimaginable pain, I remained brave and deeply honored to be by his side until his final breath.

With the support of the family, all arrangements went smoothly, and we ensured his burial in Lebanon, honoring his wishes. During the condolences, I felt a sense of peace, knowing we had fulfilled what he wanted.

A Journey Through Grief

People often saw me as strong and in control, and because of this perception, they couldn't fathom that I longed for emotional support. Yet, there were times I felt shattered, yearning for the world's hugs. Just ten months before my husband's passing, I lost my mother. While my husband fought colon cancer, my mother was suffering across the globe, and the restrictions of COVID-19 isolated me further. Juggling two profound losses simultaneously is what I call being **"Suddenly Alone."**

Unexpectedly, new connections emerged with people who sensed my deep sorrow beneath the surface. Another meaningful acquaintance I met on a business trip, noticing my pain, sent me a book to my hotel titled *Rise Up: A Widow's Journal,* which helped me begin to process my grief. I realized that true connections often arise when we allow ourselves to be genuine and vulnerable, even in our darkest moments.

I learned that no matter how much consciousness, control, or effort you invest to prevent the unexpected, life has its own plans. When my husband passed away, I was engulfed in shock—not just from the loss of my best friend, my home, and my unwavering support, but from the reactions of those around me. Despite our commitment to live our lives with integrity, my husband and I never interfered in anyone else's affairs. Yet, in the wake of his death, I found myself overwhelmed by those who felt entitled to step into my life and make decisions on my behalf.

Lost in confusion, I came to a profound realization: as a couple, we had formed a complete, unbroken circle and protected each other. When he passed, half of that circle vanished, leaving me exposed with no shield against the outside world. In that gap, it allowed others to step in and shape my choices, assuming they knew what was best for me. This intrusion felt like an entitlement—a claim over my life that I hadn't invited.

So, to anyone facing similar challenges: stand tall, step into your wisdom, and let your light shine brightly for others. Protect what matters most, embrace the grace within you, and remember—you are never truly alone. Your strength can inspire others to find their own light, even amidst the darkest days.

Grief is a process of growth. It does not define us; it refines us.

Turning Point: Decisions at Life's Crossroads

Navigating this new reality was a challenge. I've always shied away from confrontation, believing that sometimes silence speaks louder than words. But this silence became a heavy burden, drowning out my own voice amidst the chaos. It took time, reflection, and the courage to seek connection to begin piecing myself back together. I was perceived as weak because of my silence and patience.

As I surrounded myself with the right people, I began to reclaim my power. I learned to filter out the external noise—the "shoulds," "shouldn'ts," and endless "what ifs" that crowded my mind. It became clear that I had to stand tall in my truth and embrace my wisdom and values by telling everyone to **BACK OFF!**

During that period, as I delved deeply into my meditation and affirmations, I envisioned a painting three times, mirroring my inner struggles. Finally, I got up, painted it, and named it *Static Noise*. The artwork features a bold red circle at its center, surrounded by various shapes, brushstrokes, and inscriptions, capturing, and depicting the noise and pressures from society.

Faced with debts, bounced checks, court cases, and countless other struggles, I found myself completely isolated. My close circle distanced themselves from me and my children because I chose a path that didn't align with their logic or expectations. They dismissed my choices, reducing my voice to nothing.

In times of hardship, I felt compelled to tap into the essence of who I am. It was through stillness, self-awareness, and moving forward alone that I truly connected with my core and creativity. I realized that, with the greatest power—the Creator—by my side, I have all I need to live my life in freedom.

In moments of anger or frustration, I remind myself to be my own compass by asking: "Will this action bring me happiness?", "Does it align with my core values?" What matters most to me is making choices I won't regret—choices that preserve my values, inner peace, and happiness.

Yet, in that silence, a fierce determination emerged within me. With nothing left to lose, I chose to stand up for my freedom and independence—the very things I cherished when my husband was alive.

The Dance of Joy and Pain

There are times when I find myself reflecting, questioning, and wondering about the chaos that surrounds me. Hurricanes, storms, and doubts have swept through my life, urging me to slow down, embrace who I am, and create a protective barrier around my inner peace and sacred space.

In these moments of turmoil, I have also come to recognize the certainty of my capabilities and the vital messages I wish to share of hope, resilience, values, and faith, which I hold dearly to my heart and will not allow any circumstance to change who I am. I believe that God did not bring us into this world to suffer; rather, He is by our side, protecting and guiding us toward our greatness. Sometimes, God isolates us before He elevates us.

Through this journey, while continuously developing my skills and making choices, I discovered a profound truth: hope and faith are always present, even in the darkest of times. By distinguishing what matters to me, I found the strength to navigate the storms alongside my ongoing growth. Strength is not about being unbreakable; it is about bending without breaking.

I learned that while life may pull us in unexpected directions, we have the power to chart our own course. In moments of uncertainty and doubt, it's easy to succumb to fear—wanting to hide, retreat, or ignore the challenges before us. At this defining moment, I realized there are two interpretations of fear: either Forget Everything and Run or Face Everything and Rise. I chose to rise.

Choosing to rise is an invitation to dig deeper and discover the strength within us. It is embracing discomfort and confronting obstacles head-on. It has taught me valuable lessons about courage, hope, and the power of perseverance. Whenever I faced fear, I emerged stronger, wiser, and more resilient.

The unexpected trials became the catalyst for profound

change. So, I encourage you to ask yourself: When fear knocks at your door, will you run away or will you face it with courage?

My Wisdom of Believing Beyond

Through the lessons I've learned and my understanding of life, I envisioned the following:

For my life, I thought that by doing everything possible to shield my family and provide what I felt was missing when I lost my father—from the pain to the lack of support—it would be appreciated. But instead, it turned out to be hurtful and did not prevent life's unexpected detours from happening. I could have simply accepted that I did my best, acknowledged that I can't control the unknown, and allowed myself to let go.

Despite the challenges of COVID-19 restrictions, we were incredibly fortunate to receive special approval for our children to join us in Austria, even though entry was limited to residents and citizens only. That's what I call *Believing Beyond.*

At work, I believed that staying low-profile and cautious would keep me in control, taking only calculated risks. I also assumed that by being kind, generous, and trusting, I'd naturally set boundaries and avoid conflict. Yet, here I am, facing all these obstacles and hardships. I learned the hard way that gentle communication can be mistaken for weakness. I had to speak firmly and clearly, and though it was difficult, it helped me uncover and address much of the chaos around me.

But instead, the pieces of the puzzle began to fall into place. In 2022, opportunities started unfolding, guiding me to meet the right people, like Denise McCormick, an educator and multiple best-selling author, who introduced me to a collaborative book, *Dear Younger Self,* which became a number one seller on Amazon.

Back in 2015, I wanted to create a tablet for kids to enhance their creativity, build their self-esteem, and help them deal with their emotions. In 2022, while in Toronto, I met with a friend who is an app developer. I shared my vision with her, and she said, "We can develop it for you."

I developed an app for kids ages 3-9 called *Astrosteem*, designed to build self-esteem, channel emotions, and combat bullying.

Through faith, belief, resilience, surrendering, letting go, and trusting in a higher power, that's when miraculous results begin to unfold.

How Did I Do It?

Through continuous learning, maintaining a growth mindset, having the right support, pushing through my fears, trusting, stepping into the unknown, and taking the first step in faith.

Some of the invaluable daily habits and tools I practice before starting my day include meditation, gratitude, art, and exercise. These help ground me and set the tone for my day.

I focus my energy where it's necessary to fuel my mission and vision—being a beacon of hope for those who feel lost. Most importantly, I surround myself with people who inspire me rather than those who dim my light.

Whatever I considered a red line, thinking it was handled, I've concluded that God has His ways of testing our resilience, faith, and perseverance. Yet, I believe He will never give us anything we cannot handle.

God has His messages for us, which we may understand immediately, later, or perhaps never. Surrendering and trusting in His plan is key. Notice, when you fight reality, you suffer.

The unexpected trials became the catalyst for profound change.

Finding My Way Home

My journey has been shaped by a series of detours that have allowed me to focus on coaching, retreats, art, and decluttering my emotions.

I acknowledge and embrace all the obstacles I've faced, as they have helped me tap into my greatness, align with my purpose, and give the benefit of the doubt in every situation.

By staying true to myself, I nurture my youthful spirit,

boundless energy, and playful nature despite the challenges I encounter. Through creative expressions like art, journaling, dancing with joy, and cherishing the beauty in life's smallest moments, I've created a magnetic force that attracts the right opportunities and people into my life.

After my husband's death, someone close to me said, "At your age, you need to slow down." It felt like the finale, as if it were the end. But this is a new season in my life, and I choose to live beyond limits and labels—I'm not done yet!

Rising Through Challenges: A Journey of Growth and Resilience

Moving forward, my mission is to share these lessons and tools with others who may feel overwhelmed by life's challenges, helping them channel their emotions and discover their own coping mechanisms.

By sharing my journey, I remind myself that I am not alone and my adversity could be someone else's survival guide.

Remember: Life is not happening *to* us; it is happening *for* us to grow.

Life is a constant dance between joy and pain. We can't always control the music life plays, but we can choose how we dance to it.

God, please grant me the courage to change what I can, the serenity to accept what I cannot, and the wisdom to know the difference as I trust Your guidance.

ABOUT RAIDA ABDULSALAM ABU-ISSA

Raida was born in Qatar, grew up in Lebanon and London, and lived in Paris before returning to Qatar. Growing up in diverse cultures taught her adaptability and resilience. A psychology class sparked her interest in child psychology, focusing on understanding emotions and overcoming limiting beliefs.

An entrepreneur at heart, Raida has successfully launched projects in entertainment, the arts, and food and beverage after leaving her family business. She is a Barrett Values and Jack Canfield Success Principles Certified Trainer, a growth mindset coach and artist. Raida contributed to Dear Younger Self, a #1 bestselling collaborative book exploring themes of hope, grief, and resilience.

Raida's mission is to empower others to manage emotions, diffuse triggers, and unlock their full potential. She offers women 1:1 and group coaching, and facilitates transformative retreats in Austria, incorporating hikes, yoga, art therapy, and workshops. Through her work, Raida creates spaces for women to reconnect with themselves and nature, helping them discover their inner resilience and growth potential.

"Life is a dance of joy and pain. I'm the light that refuses to surrender."
Life ends when you stop dreaming.
Hope ends when you stop believing.
Love ends when you stop caring.

To connect with Raida

Instagram: @raida_abdulsalam
Email: raida.bitar@aljedad.com

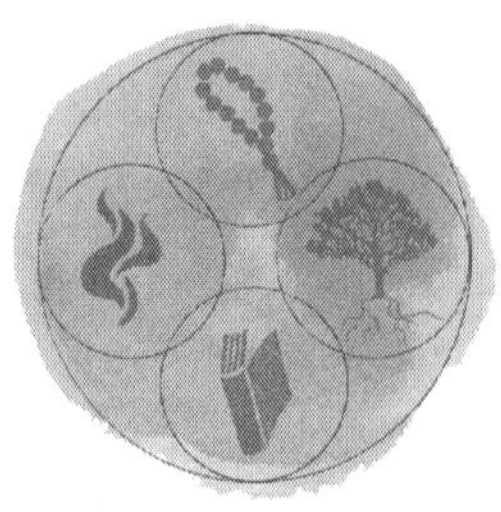

MY WISH FOR YOU

Dr. Lucette Beall

What does Believe Beyond mean to you? To me, it means when you can believe beyond anything you previously could have imagined and then you can sustain that belief and do or create things that you never dreamed were possible before. `The first time I found myself in a situation where I needed to Believe Beyond was when I found myself on the heels of a divorce in which I did not ask for child support. I was a self-employed professional (veterinarian) with no paid sick days, facing fifteen months of cancer treatment including multiple surgeries, six rounds of chemotherapy, and seven weeks of daily radiation. Every time I was not physically in the building, we were not making money, and I was the sole financial support for myself and my daughter.

I was determined to beat the cancer AND to survive financially. To not drown in fear and overwhelm, I had to BELIEVE and TRUST in a way that I had never known before. Every day required this BELIEF. I learned to trust that whatever I needed that day or that week, whether it was a ride to an activity for my daughter or money to pay for necessities or appointments to sustain the business or the discernment for treatment decisions, it would show up. I learned to completely let go of worry and fear and believe and trust in ways that I had never experienced before. It was important to bring my focus in as tight as necessary to release the overwhelm—even if that was simply what do I need to do in the next five minutes…because thinking bigger than that was too much in the moment. I believe this experience set me up for what was coming next in my life.

Almost a year and a half after I finished cancer treatment, my brother suffered a severe traumatic brain injury in a freak horse accident. He was not supposed to live, then he was not supposed to wake up from his coma, he started waking up from the coma, the medical team said he would never leave an institution, and they did not hold out much hope that he would ever walk and talk again. My brother defied all the odds and learned to walk and talk and even got his driver's license reinstated. However, he still had many challenges because he had suffered damage in all areas of his brain. Two years after the accident, he found himself in a state mental hospital in the middle of a divorce with no one to help him. Without someone to take him in and help him with all the things he still couldn't manage, he was destined to spend the rest of his life in that mental hospital.

The day I found out that he had been put in the state mental hospital, I felt something so strong deep within me telling me I HAD to find a way to help him. I had been talking to him over the past months, and I knew he was struggling and trying so hard to figure it out. I was not in the financial position to just step out of my business, but to help him, that is what I would have to do. My banker, my parents, and other trusted advisors were all in agreement that this was not something I should do. But deep inside, I could not deny the feeling that I was absolutely supposed to do whatever it took to help him and give him a chance to live his life outside of that state mental institution. I simply could not imagine walking away and leaving him to that terrible fate. I do believe my experience while going through cancer treatment and still running my business gave me the courage to step up for my brother in such a big way.

The day I found out that he was in the state mental institution, I left my business, went home, packed a suitcase, and drove straight to Norman, OK. I got a hotel room and went to work, learning everything I could about his entire situation. I interviewed his psychiatrist, his counselor, his wife, and everyone intimately involved with him. I poured over his records from his previous stays that year at private mental hospitals that my parents had paid for. I was looking for the missing pieces to help him. I would go to sleep in the hotel room and wake up in a few hours with ideas and puzzle pieces coming together in my mind, and I would write them down in a notebook I kept right there next to me. I would go back to sleep, and then it would happen again. At that time, he had a temper, and with his frontal lobe damage, he was struggling to control his actions when his temper flared. I needed to make sure it would be safe to bring him home to my house. I also had to figure out how I was going to manage the financial side of things.

My medical knowledge was very helpful in this process, and as I poured over all the medical and mental health records and listened to everyone talk about the different incidents and challenges, I was able to formulate a plan and feel that I could safely bring him home to my house and give him the support he needed to regain his independence. This did not solve the financial situation for me but one of the ideas that had come to me in my sleep was to reach out to his former boss, Jay Scaramucci. He is an incredible man who had been very supportive of my brother for the entire two years following his accident, and he had the resources to help me. I asked for a loan, which he granted me with a very low interest rate. He did tell me at the time that he thought stepping out of my business would be very difficult financially but that he would provide the loan and give me a chance to help my brother.

In August, two years almost to the day of my brother's accident, we moved him to my house, and the next chapter of our lives began. There were many skills he still needed to learn to be as independent as possible. I also needed to get him new doctors, a psychiatrist, counselor, and so on. I also needed to get him on disability. There were also the challenges that come with a grown man who had been a boss, a mover, and a shaker, who now finds himself in the position of needing help and being unable to do many things himself or have control over his own life. There were many challenging moments, including him almost burning the house down by leaving a pan on a hot burner, having several vehicular accidents (I'm not sure how he kept his license), my daughter and I having to go find him in the middle of the night, and so much more. But through it all, he maintained his sweet nature and his appreciation for the opportunity to live life outside of the mental hospital. We were so blessed with beautiful people to love and support us all through the changes and challenges. We had many dear church friends that were there for us. He had a dear college friend and his wife, who lived fairly close to us and whom John would visit on some weekends, which gave my daughter and me some much-needed breathing space. I was a member of the Lake Ray Roberts Rotary Club, and they allowed my sweet brother to become a member there even though he would never be able to be an officer. He LOVED the Rotary Club and made many friends there, and he had one sweet friend, Dick Bullwinkle who took him on trail rides, which they both loved!!

After a little over a year, I was able to move my brother into his own small apartment and give him more of his independence back. I was still paying his bills and helping him in many ways, but he had acquired enough skills to at least live in his own space again, which he really appreciated.

I did not step foot in my practice for six weeks after I stepped out to find a way to assist my brother in his time of need. Then I began working once a week and then once or twice a week as we were able to get him settled in and doing better. After I moved him into his own apartment, I was able to go back to work full-time in the practice.

However, there were many challenges from leaving the practice for that long, and the financial situation was difficult. I had even sold my house to continue to be able to help my brother. I found myself hearing the words of my banker, my parents, Jay Scaramucci, and others and feeling like a failure because I was struggling financially from stepping out of my business to help my brother, and as he was beginning to do better, I was struggling.

For three years, I worked and struggled, feeling overwhelmed and inadequate. I got behind on payroll taxes, I missed some of my payments to Jay, I was behind to all my suppliers and struggling to pay the bills. Jay did not owe me anything, and he threatened to call the note if I did not get the payments caught up in a specific time period. I had to sit down and really evaluate my situation, and I had to decide if I was willing to go bankrupt and give up the business I had loved and nurtured for seventeen years. The day I sat down to really think this through and make a choice, I made up my mind that I was not going to go bankrupt. I decided, finally, to BELIEVE BEYOND for MYSELF and from that day forward, I changed my thinking and my thought process. This is when I began the process of understanding my Point of Power. In ONE YEAR, I went from several hundred thousand dollars in debt to almost out of debt once I made up my mind and started taking back my Point of Power. Eight months later, I made a large down payment on my current home. I went on to build a seven-figure business.

However, the clinic had reached a point where I would need to step more into management and away from the daily practice of medicine and interacting with clients to take it to the next level. In the meantime, my heart and soul were calling me in a much different direction. As I grew through the challenges both mentally and financially in stepping out to help my brother and all that followed, I began to find myself called in the direction of helping, sharing, and teaching others about their own Point of Power and all of the incredible knowledge and tools that I had gained through the challenges that had allowed me to go from almost bankrupt to paying off several hundred thousand dollars in debt in such a short period of time. And to go from doubt, fear, and inadequacy to confident, believing, and receiving.

In meditation one morning, it came to me that I was supposed to write a book entitled, *How to Build an Extra-Ordinary Life at Any Age*. At the time, I did not understand it, but the thought was so clear and persistent that I wrote it down. I literally stood in the kitchen at one point asking God, the Universe, "What are you talking about? Why me?" The answer was so clear, "If not you, then who?" Until you claim your own worthiness, your own Point of Power, how can you share and give it others?"

Over the course of the next year, all the pieces of an *Extra-Ordinary Life* began to unfold, and I came to understand that it is about knowing how to choose to live from the inside out—NOT from the outside in as we are so often taught in society. How to learn to thrive in any situation, how to BELIEVE in yourself. How to KNOW that not only are you worthy (we all are) but that YOU, yes YOU, can thrive in any situation and with the right tools every challenge has a silver lining or a golden opportunity just waiting for you to BELIEVE in it and yourself and take your life to the next level. Understanding your Point of Power and learning to recognize when you are giving it away to others is key to gaining the resilience and belief to carry you through every challenge and create opportunities for yourself.

As all this unfolded, it became clear that it was time to sell my practice, not to retire but to move fully into my next calling, my next adventure, the Extra-Ordinary Life I was being called to without knowing yet how it was going to unfold. This calling is one in which Believing Beyond is not just for Extra-Ordinary challenges as I had previously believed. Instead, Believing Beyond has become a way of life, and the opportunity is to live an Extra-Ordinary Life EVERY DAY. Within six months of deciding to sell my practice the deal was done.

Ten years after I first stepped out of my practice and a month after I made the final note payment to Jay Scaramucci for the privilege of helping my brother, Extra-Ordinary Life began to take off with personal mindset and life coaching, speaking, workshops, videos, books, and so much more. I found myself preparing for a workshop in Indiana for a conference for adult educators. In the hotel room that morning I went to pull the curtains back for some sunshine, only to be met with darkness and heavy fog. As I turned, I saw my phone on the nightstand, and a beautiful picture of the sun's rays shining magnificently through trees was on the phone. A picture I did not take nor had ever seen before. At the same time, I realized that a song by Rascal Flatts, "My Wish," was playing on my phone, which was on my usual Pandora station (not country and I have never heard this song before or since on this station). I immediately knew it was a message for me.

But it was only later when I found out my brother had passed away peacefully at home the night before I received the message, that I understood with such clarity (and lots of tears) that this beautiful message was from my brother. The words in the song perfectly signified his love and support that was always there, and the image of him supporting me and dreaming big for me now. Oh how my heart both ached and was so very full at the same time. It was and still is, a smile through your tears moment in time.

And so, we have come full circle! I loved and supported my brother and grew so much in my ability to BELIEVE BEYOND to be able to step out and help him. In return, I became more than I ever could have imagined and so much of who I get to be today is related to our relationship and the gift of having him as a brother and stepping up for him. In the financial challenges I faced stepping out to help him, I truly learned what my Point of Power is and when I am giving it away and how to get it back.

And now he is healed, and he is free, and he is there for me in a way he couldn't be these last twelve years. He was always my biggest cheerleader, and he still is, from a different vantage point. My wish for you is that you come to understand your Point of Power and seek to take it back when you give it away. That you know from the core of your being that you are one hundred percent worthy of an Extra-Ordinary Life and you are willing to be brave enough to live it!! All my love! Dr. Lucette

ABOUT DR. LUCETTE BEALL

Dr. Lucette is a dynamic public speaker, coach, author and visionary course creator dedicated to transforming lives. With her innovative approach, Dr. Lucette unlocks the secrets of personal development and cognitive behavioral strategies. Her journey of resilience and transformation serves as a beacon of hope. From being a single mother facing divorce without child support to battling cancer and financial hardship, she emerged as a triumphant example of turning adversity into victory. Driven by her unique philosophy on life, she invites you to embrace life's challenges as opportunities, to rewrite your story, and to live with intention and choice. She has three decades of experience as a veterinarian and business owner as well as being an international speaker and co-author of two internationally best-selling books. She has created a dynamic and robust subscription program to give you the opportunity to have the tools to live from the inside out and create your own Extra-Ordinary Life! FREE 30 DAY TRIAL! You can find more info here: https://www.drlucette.net/your-extra-ordinary-life-community-with-dr-lucette

To connect with Lucette

Website: http://www.drlucette.net
Facebook: https://www.facebook.com/drlucettebeall
Instagram: https://www.instagram.com/drlucette

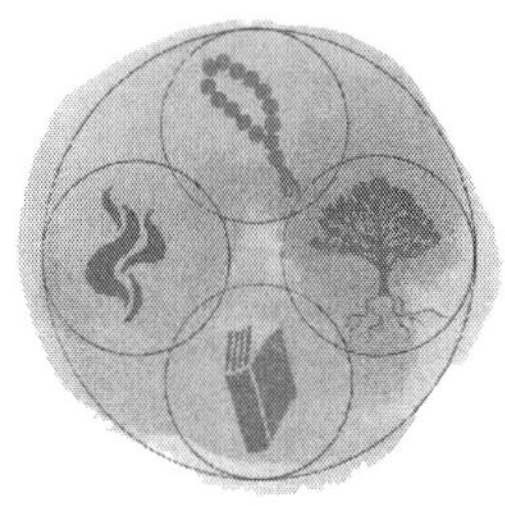

TURN SURVIVING TO THRIVING: RECLAIMING YOUR POWER AND PURPOSE

Ada Jenness Keller, PharmD

Have you ever felt like it might be too dramatic to admit you're merely surviving most days—not because you're facing a life-or-death situation, like being chased by a bear or caught in a raging river, but because life itself has become a test of endurance, with every single day feeling like a battle to keep your head above water? Somehow, life becomes a relentless cycle of just getting by, leaving you wondering, *"When did simply surviving replace truly living?"*

I found myself in April 2021, feeling lost, numb, and shattered questioning how my life had unraveled. My professional and personal life lay in ruins, and I was desperate to summon the strength to endure it all. Reaching that breaking point of despair wasn't sudden; it was a slow unraveling. Looking back, I see the subtle nudges, the louder warnings, and finally the moment the rug was pulled out from under me, forcing me to face my reality. I can pinpoint three turning points that not only shattered my illusions of control but ultimately pushed me to prioritize my well-being and reclaim the direction of my life. I had spent years going through the motions, buried in endless responsibilities, while joy and fulfillment quietly slipped away. I hadn't realized how easy it was to settle into survival mode and how quickly you can convince yourself that just getting by is good enough.

For most of my life, I was fortunate to face little adversity. My childhood was beautiful—filled with love, safety, and a close-knit family that instilled strong values. However, in my mid-20s, challenges began testing my resilience and faith. Heartache and grief shook my family to its core as we faced the struggles of loved ones battling addiction and loss, teaching me firsthand how precious life truly is. Yet, amidst the tragedy, there were also blessings. During this time, I graduated from pharmacy school and began my career as a pharmacist. I married my high school sweetheart, bought a home, and welcomed two wonderful children into my life. Life seemed almost picture-perfect—until my 30s brought deeply personal trials that made me question my beliefs, identity and purpose deeply.

The first significant turning point in my life occurred one summer evening in 2019, with what I initially thought was heartburn that quickly spiraled into a medical emergency. A tingling sensation down my left arm led to crushing chest pain so intense I could barely breathe. Within minutes, I was on the ground, crippled, with every muscle in my body fully tensed up. My husband rushed me to the hospital saving my life, where I was diagnosed with critically low potassium levels. Hours later, I was discharged without any answers. How could I live with the possibility of this randomly happening again and no clear way to prevent it? Instead of relief, I was consumed by anger and fear. I had to make a choice: I could continue to live in fear or control what I could. I chose to take back control where I realistically could and started with the basics of healthy living—exercise and nutrition. I committed to an in-home workout program, and movement became my lifeline. The physical activity released the anxiety and tension that had built up over years. With each step, I began to reclaim my confidence, a sense of control and trust with my body again, and peace of mind that I would be ok.

A second major turning point came in 2020 when I faced unexpected challenges in my professional life. The COVID-19 pandemic hit full force and transformed my pharmacy career overnight. I was suddenly managing not only medications but the overwhelming fear, confusion, and uncertainty of a public health crisis. The already overwhelming demands in the pharmacy intensified and grew, stretching entire pharmacy teams to their breaking point. I gave everything I had to those I served, even as the demands drained me. On my days off though, I often found myself in recovery mode and struggling to fully recharge. It wasn't just the effects of the pandemic draining my energy and well-being at work. Unforeseen traumas surfaced as well. One evening, I found myself helping a technician who was held at gunpoint during a prescription delivery. I intervened in life-or-death crises, like performing CPR and administering Narcan to save a young woman who had been thrown from her drug dealer's car and left for dead outside the pharmacy. While I managed to help in those extreme moments, the emotional weight of those experiences was both heavy and taxing. I brought my tears and anxiety home to my supportive husband, who, through no fault of his own, couldn't fix what I was going through. I continued to convince myself that I was strong enough to endure the unhealthy mental and emotional toll of my career choice.

As I entered into January 2021, the line between my professional and personal life blurred in ways I could no longer control or manage. It began with a regular customer whose behavior escalated from inappropriate comments to outright sexual harassment. From the moment he confessed his supposed love for me, my intuition urged me to document every incident. I firmly set a boundary, telling him his behavior was unacceptable and could not continue. He would retreat for a bit, only to return with more brazen advances. Despite warnings from myself and my staff, he persisted, skirting direct threats but leaving me on edge. Deep down, I worried my corporate leaders wouldn't take my concerns seriously to change anything.

On March 14, 2021, months of harassment reached a final breaking point. The day began as a quiet Sunday shift with just me and a young male technician working in the pharmacy. Suddenly, angry yelling erupted from the front of the store. I looked up to see a man grabbing one of my coworkers by the shirt, screaming obscenities and threats in his face. My stomach dropped when I realized it was him, the man who had been harassing me. Within moments, he let go of the employee but stormed toward the pharmacy. My heart sank as he approached the counter, his voice booming with obscenities and threats to harm me. What had started as verbal and sexual harassment had escalated into an immediate threat to my safety. My hands shook as I reached for the phone to call the police, but I was acutely aware of how vulnerable I was! Trapped in the pharmacy, I knew he could easily climb over the counter—or worse, simply walk around it—to get to me.

Years of experience had taught me to stay professional under pressure, but this was different. This wasn't about calming an irate customer; I was being personally and directly targeted. Forcing myself to stay calm, I made him aware that the police were on their way, hoping that he would leave. I didn't dare show fear or say anything that might escalate his irrational anger further. He left before the police arrived, but my sense of safety had vanished. Shortly after that initial incident, I made a second call when he returned back to the store. The police ended up encountering him this second time. However, instead of removing him from the premises, they escorted him back to the pharmacy to check for a prescription. Standing just feet from me, with an officer beside him, he yelled obscenities at me angrily again. The officer warned him to calm down, but the absurdity of the moment wasn't lost on me. There I was, serving the very man who had just threatened my safety after months of sexual harassment. I complied, hoping to avoid giving him any excuse to return, knowing I still had hours left on my shift where I felt very alone to protect myself.

Not surprisingly, he returned later that day and again the very next day—eight times overall! Twice, he attempted to apologize directly to me, but the fear and anxiety his presence brought were inescapable. He could walk in whenever he pleased, while I felt trapped behind the counter like a sitting duck. The constant stream of patient needs required my full attention, yet I was anxious and afraid, knowing this man could—and did—appear at any moment. I felt trapped, forced to continue working because of my financial obligations, personal responsibilities, and years of investment in my career. I continued to work my shifts despite feeling scared and powerless as I waited for updates from corporate. I had expected my employer to take swift action to ensure my safety after the escalating incidents, but instead found myself begging and demanding for a resolution. It took nearly two excruciating weeks of persistent requests for action before corporate leaders officially banned him from the store.

As I fought desperately for a safe working environment while managing the extreme emotional and mental stress surrounding work, a third defining and pivotal area of my life was unraveling simultaneously. My mother had been battling ovarian cancer for several years, but her health had been quickly declining since that January as well. She had experienced an emergency surgery while in the hospital during this same time period. I visited her in the hospital to check on her, but it would be the very last time that I would be able to speak to her. To our shock and surprise, during the quick transition of leaving her room to switch places with my father, the medical team placed her in an emergency medically induced coma on a ventilator. Days went by questioning if she would come back to us. Doctors took her off the ventilator and informed us that she would have only days left with us.

My mother passed away about a week later, on April 3, 2021. Grief consumed me. My life had spiraled to an unrecognizable state, and the loss of my mother, the woman who was my rock, left me in the darkest, saddest place I had ever known. As women, we often feel the need to hold everything together despite our struggles, but I had to allow myself to grieve deeply to heal from so much trauma. In the midst of this heartache, I remembered how supportive and essential self-care was to my well-being. The day she died, I saw myself standing at a pivotal crossroads. I realized I had a choice: I could fall into a dark depression or I could take steps to save myself and mirror my mother's qualities of strength and resilience.

I chose to lean on the one thing that had grounded and supported me since back in 2019: physical movement and my growing interest in building a healthier mindset. Despite my fragile emotions, I made a commitment to a 100-day workout program starting the day she passed away. This daily practice became my lifeline, a deliberate act of self-care, self-love, and healing. Each day, I showed up for myself, taking control of the one thing I could when key areas of my life felt like destruction. Through movement, I began reclaiming my strength and spirit. I reframed my circumstances as a chance to grow, reminding myself that while this dark chapter could break me, I had the power to rise above it just the same.

In a newly empowered and healthier state, I vowed to live beyond mere survival, daring to dream bigger and brighter. I worked on releasing the heaviness of the previous years and envisioned a calmer pharmacy where I could efficiently care and support those in need. Barely a month after my mother's passing, my wish was granted with an unexpected transfer offer. Without hesitation, I embraced the chance to leave the toxic environment that had drained me. By June, I stepped into a new pharmacy, guided by the power of movement and mindset, determined to build a healthier and more empowered life onward.

Looking back, I now see that those years of enduring some of my hardest personal challenges weren't the defining end of my story or my destruction. A dark chapter can become an opportunity to recognize what no longer serves us on our path. It gives us the chance to choose a new direction—one that supports our health, happiness, and well-being. I now understand that my darkest chapters were substantial turning points in my journey, and for that, I am truly grateful. I discovered the profound connection and transformative power between moving my body and shifting my mindset to live life as I desire. Each workout became a victory—an opportunity to release built-up stress and shift stagnant energy, while also allowing loving light to seep back into my soul. Each mindset practice created space for more self-love, healing, and awareness, enabling me to better listen to and guide myself from within. Since embracing these practices, life has unfolded in ways I once only imagined and desired.

Often, the lessons buried in our struggles only become clear once we are past them and out of survival mode. To expand and dream bigger, we must first feel safe. By nurturing our bodies through movement, reframing our mindset, and embracing practices such as affirmations, gratitude, manifestation, resetting beliefs, and visualization, we can shift from survival mode to a life filled with meaning, fulfillment, and calm, purposeful intention. No matter how heavy life feels, you have the power to reclaim and reignite your innate strength. We never lose our divine ability to create the life we envision and desire—it's simply a choice whether or not to wield that power!

As you consider your own life, think about the chapters you've faced that felt overwhelming or impossible. Perhaps you, too, have endured moments that left you questioning your strength. Remember, experiencing those moments doesn't make you weak—it makes you human! Your darkest chapter never has to be your whole defining story. Make it a turning point instead!

You can embrace a new, empowering path forward—one that leads to *thriving*, not just simply surviving through life!

I'd be honored to help guide you through discovering practical, healthy, and powerful tools that you can implement in your daily life to create more peace, joy, and personal fulfillment! You can find the tools and resources that have helped me continue on a thriving path forward at www.turnsurvivingtothriving.com, as well as ways to work with me one-on-one. My wish is that you apply the same loving and empowering tools to give yourself a chance to create divine magic in your life as well! We cannot always control the challenging circumstances that life presents to us, but we can always find our strength and courage from within in to navigate *through* them and *beyond* them! If I could rise from my darkest days more empowered and vibrant, so can you! Are you ready to let go of simply surviving and turn toward *thriving* instead?!

ABOUT ADA JENNESS KELLER, PHARMD

Jenness is a certified life coach specializing in combining movement and mindset practices to help women transition from merely surviving to truly thriving. With over a decade of experience as a retail pharmacist, she understands the toll high-stress environments take on mental, physical, and spiritual well-being. Her passion lies in empowering women, particularly those in demanding healthcare careers, to rediscover their personal power, cultivate inner peace, and create fulfilling lives.

Having personally faced burnout, profound grief, and health challenges, Jenness brings deep compassion and insight to her work. Her journey from offering one-on-one pharmacy consultations to mentoring women through coaching stems from her mission to guide others out of survival mode. She provides practical strategies, personalized tools, courses, and heartfelt support through her website, www.turnsurvivingtothriving.com, helping her clients design lives they love—both inside *and* outside of work!

Her greatest joys and blessings come from being a wife to her best friend, a mother to their two beautiful children, and serving with love and light. She treasures self-care, lifelong learning, and the wisdom nature offers us all. Her work reflects her unwavering commitment to helping others reclaim peace, purpose, and joy in both their personal and professional lives.

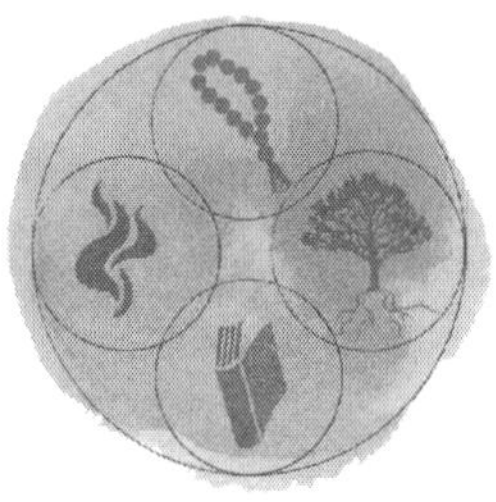

IT WASN'T IN THE PLANS

Viktoriya Legkun

Do you know what it feels like to be living the dream? Let me paint you a picture of mine. I was in my 20's, just recently married, working at a dream job, and starting my own online business. My life was far from perfect but it was perfect to me. The weekends were spent with family, laughing while we traveled, and the weekdays were filled with learning new skills and growing in my education. I began mapping out what my future would look like with excitement and planning for my next big move in life. I had plans and an incredible belief that everything I wanted was falling into place.

But here's the thing, nobody ever plans for disaster in life. Nobody gets ready for their world to be turned completely upside down. Looking back now, I understand it wasn't as perfect as I believed it to be. My body was already trying to speak to me; it was quietly already talking to me through subtle symptoms that something wasn't right. But what 20-year-old actually stops and thinks—-"Could I really be sick?" I know that thought never even crossed my mind. I was young. I was invincible, or so I thought.

At first, it began very quietly. Almost unnoticeable. Sometimes a lingering fatigue that wouldn't lift. Then a headache that would last longer than normal. Random pains throughout my body that I couldn't explain. I came up with every excuse at first. I probably didn't get enough sleep. I didn't drink enough water today. I've been more stressed at work than usual. With every new symptom, I found a new excuse to justify it. I tried to silence my body. I tried to put my symptoms in a box. I didn't want to deal with it. I *shouldn't* have to deal with it! What was I even dealing with? I didn't want to know. But the problem with that is just because you want something painful to stop doesn't mean it will listen. And mine was just getting louder and louder.

After months of enduring chronic pain, I finally became desperate enough to go see a doctor. You know what the funny thing is? I fully had the belief that I would walk into that doctor's office, get some tests done, take some medicine, and I would go right back to my life. That ended up being far from my reality. One doctor visit became two, and two became three, and three became thirty. My subtly quiet symptoms became debilitating pain in every part of my body. I would wake up in pain. In the span of one day, I would usually experience more than 10 symptoms. I went to every specialist imaginable. I flew to different countries to get answers. As time went on, I began feeling less like a human and more like a lab rat. And every single test would come back just like the last, inconclusive. My whole world shrank, and everything revolved around my illness.

This went on for ten long years. I would wake up in fear of what the day had to bring. I would get through each day just praying for night to come so I could go to sleep and stop feeling pain, and the worst part was, I would go to bed, unable to fall asleep no matter how tired I was. I lived in a body that was torturing me. It played cruel jokes on me. Mind games. I could be okay one second and passing out the next. I could eat something I'd eaten a thousand times before, and this time it would send my body in hives. I began to fear absolutely everything. Eating, sleeping, new products, staying in, going out. It all came with a moment of pain and a memory that would stay embedded in my head for years to come. I was a prisoner of my own life. No matter how difficult it became physically, I kept striving to figure it out. I knew something was really wrong. I felt it in every fiber of my being.

After years of hospitals and thousands of tests, doctors began to call it "The Mystery Illness." I could see they gave up. I was no longer just battling a disease; I was battling the very people who were supposed to be helping me. I began hearing words like "hypochondriac, anxiety, depression, postpartum, eccentric, dramatic." I lost my health, and now I had professionals telling me that it was all in my mind.

We've all heard the phrase "Hitting rock bottom." I had heard it many times. The problem is, I never realized that when you get there, you break into a million pieces. I questioned everything. I was bedbound physically, and after years of no answers, I was completely knocked down mentally and emotionally. I looked in the mirror and didn't recognize the person staring back at me. Life had stolen everything away from me. I was in pain physically. I was mentally anxious and depressed. I was emotionally so hurt that everyone gave up on me. If you've ever felt a pain so deep that it quite literally hurts your soul, your whole being, that's what I was in. I was in unimaginable physical, mental, and emotional pain. It was the darkest tunnel I had ever been through, and I wouldn't wish it on my worst enemy.

There was one day I remember laying on the floor in my room. It was a gloomy day outside. I could hear the raindrops hitting the roof so loudly. Every drop felt like it was pounding against my head. My husband sat across the room, just staring at me. He didn't know what to say anymore. All the words had been said. I could hear my kids running around on the outside of the door. I had no strength left. I was exhausted, and I was done. I had no more fight left in me. Then I saw my son's fingers squeeze through the cracks, his little fingers wiggling. I heard him quietly say, "Mommy, come play with us." At that moment, I looked up at my husband. His face was so pale, so tired. I could see he was so broken up inside; despite his best efforts, he didn't know how to help me anymore. In that moment, I made a decision. No matter how long it took, no matter how many people called me "crazy," no matter how weak and tired I was, I wouldn't give up. I would fight until I got answers. I would fight when I had no fight left in me. I would fight for myself, I would fight for my kids, I would fight for my husband, and I would fight for every single person out there who would one day go through what I went through. I would fight. I would win. And I would help others get out of the dark tunnel. It was no longer a question; it was a statement. I would beat this. I would win.

As the months went by, I would love to say that things got better and I quickly got answers, but that would be a lie. Despite my best efforts, I became much worse. But I kept fighting. Through every painful day, I searched. I looked for answers; I tried healing my body to the best of my efforts; I tried to live life to the best of my abilities at that point. Although I was feeling much worse, my mindset had completely shifted. I no longer allowed myself to have the thoughts of surrendering to my pain. I reconstructed every thought to winning. I was in battle, and one day I would win. That was now my new truth. It was no longer an "If"; it was a matter of when.

One day, we were out at the beach with the whole family. It was a beautiful sunny day. The only place I felt full peace was by the ocean. It always gave me a peace beyond my understanding. When the ocean was so vast, my problems stopped feeling so large. As I walked back to the lobby of the hotel, we gathered our things and walked over to the local restaurant for lunch. Dozens of kids yelling with joy, our friends laughing over the activities of the day, the sun shining through my sunglasses. It was a moment I'll never forget. I opened the door to the restaurant, and in one foul moment, it was gone. I opened the door and walked into the restaurant, and a moment of shock just washed over me. Was I dreaming? Was it in my head? Possibly, I wasn't understanding something. But no, it was all too real. As the kids ran to their seats and the loudness of everyone washed over the restaurant, I quietly took my seat. My husband, laughing at a joke coming from across the table, looked over at me. Realizing I wasn't laughing, he leaned over to me and said, "Are you okay?" I quietly looked over at him, in a frozen, almost emotionless way, and said, "I think I just lost my eyesight in my left eye; it's gone."

For me, this was the last straw. I wasn't sad. I wasn't broken. I was angry, and I was done. I was done allowing others to tell me what my life was going to look like. I was done allowing my body to steal my joy. God gave me peace. And I found a strength that I didn't even think was possible before. I had to keep going. I had to fight. I went down every rabbit hole looking for answers. I had doctors tell me I was out of my mind. I had inspectors tell me it was in my head. I had friends tell me I had to accept this was my new way of life. But let me tell you something. You can have a million people telling you that you're wrong, but if you have that inner feeling deep inside that is urging you, like a silent scream, listen to it. So many people fight that inner feeling, but if you really listen to it, it can unlock a strength within you you never knew you had. So often we are told to calm down. To stay silent. But each of us has a fire within us that we should never silence or quench.

I didn't calm down. And because of that, after a decade of pain, I finally figured it out. After dozens of doctors told me it wasn't possible, three home inspectors told me nothing was there, I finally decided to get myself tested for mycotoxin illness. My results came back astronomically high. There it was; a decade of illness, and the answer was right there in front of me, on a paper. Eventually, we kept searching and finally found out that our home was riddled with mold. The previous owner had flooded the house, and it was never taken care of, just painted over.

I spent the next years of my life healing both physically and mentally. I was no longer the same person I was ten years ago. I was like a vase that had broken many times into millions of little pieces. But I was slowly putting it all back together again. Yes, I would never look like I did before, but the thing about broken vases—when you shine a light on them, they make the most beautiful light. The patterns scatter all around the room with the most unique blend of light. I wasn't the same person I used to be, but through my brokenness, my pain, my resilience, I am now able to shine a light all over the world and help others who need it. I am able to empower others, find a voice, find a purpose, and truly thrive in life. Remember—life's difficulties do not define you; they just give you the wings to soar higher than you ever imagined.

Remember—life's difficulties do not define you; they just give you the wings to soar higher than you ever imagined.

ABOUT VIKTORIYA LEGKUN

Viktoriya Legkun is a Best-Selling Author, a Health and Wellness Advocate, a Speaker, and a passionate Business and Life Coach. Viktoriya is the creator of NaturallyViktoriya on social media, empowering thousands with her message of wellness and resilience. She has grown an online business platform teaching creators to use their knowledge and message to create online businesses. Viktoriya is also the founder of the Thriving After Trauma Philosophy TM, which helps people RENEW their life after living through trauma and pain.

Viktoriya's clients have been able to find purpose in life and create impact-driven businesses using her story and knowledge. She also has been able to guide clients to finding resilience and a passion for life after they have gone through hurdles that life has thrown at them.

To learn more about how you can connect and work with Viktoriya, you can visit her website at www.viktoriya-legkun.com, where you can find various ways to access her transformational strategies through programs, books, and free products.

Make sure to visit the website and grab your FREE gifts today! Are you ready to change your life?

To connect with Viktoriya

www.viktoriya-legkun.com
info@viktoriya-legkun.com
Instagram: @viktoriya_legkun & naturallyviktoriya
Facebook: Viktoriya Legkun

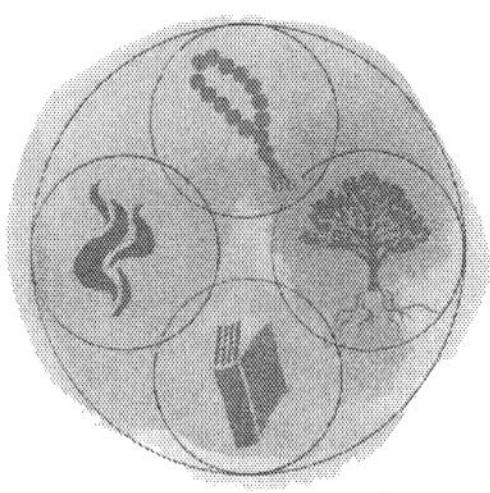

THE ESSENCE OF THINGS

Barbara Lanz

This is a story about us and objects. Deep down, I've always sensed that there is life in every solid thing we surround ourselves with. Naturally enough, this also has to do with physics and how things are made from elements and atoms, respectively, which all move and vibrate at different rates, but this is not the point right now. Instead, I mean the essence of things, the sparkling soul of objects, and their importance to us.

The history of the world, and hence your and my history as part of the evolution of mankind, is inextricably linked to objects and their quality.

"Quality" serves as an umbrella term for everything relevant to an item and its production process. It is comprised of aspects such as material properties, execution, performance, reliability, longevity, and safety. The higher the quality of an object, the more life, the more essence, it possesses.

For some of our earlier cultures, bare survival depended on quality. Imagine hunting for food with a bow and arrow and the bow breaks due to poor construction. Or carrying home fresh water in a jug that leaks. Or exploring new territories in vessels that won't make the journey because the shipwrights didn't do their jobs properly. Since objects and their nature truly mattered back then, our relationship with those very objects was a close and highly appreciative one. After all, their essence meant safety, meant life, and our liaison represented a highly meaningful exchange of energy. Therefore, we took proper care, maintained, repaired, and only replaced if there was no other way.

Of course, things changed over time and comfort first replaced sheer survival, then necessity. The more comfort has been increasing and objects piling up, the less we feel connected to what we surround ourselves with.

For decades now we have been picking our commodities from an embarrassment of riches and slowly but steadily have started to blindly rely on a constant market overstock of literally everything that is out there. Our beds of roses are overflowing with roses that hardly smell anymore. Numbly drowning in easy-access possessions we neither question nor need, we've long lost the sense of what truly matters to us. What makes us connect with our essence and how we can feel our most authentic self. Instead, we are so focused on itemizing our own unique style that we completely ignore that oversupply and 'what's trending right now,' in fact, accommodate the masses. There's nothing unique about that.

Certainly, our emotions always add value, no matter what. After all, emotions are *energy in motion,* but we can do better than that. We must do better than that. We owe ourselves a life of awareness, gratitude, and the conscious expression of our authenticity on a continuous basis. We are truly unique; there's no second version of us out there. So why not question the singularity around us? And this is exactly the point where the circle has come full stop. Our lives depend on quality once more. To live and express an elevated version of ourselves, we need to focus on our evolvement and celebrate our uniqueness. A successful way of doing so is to raise our awareness and appreciation of what we surround ourselves with, including the objects that shape and create our tangible environment. The more essence they contain, the higher the frequency they possess. By appreciating this fact, we raise our own vibration considerably. Put quality before quantity, and you will experience not only a mind shift but, over time, a deeper connection with yourself. If you truly connect with something else, you automatically connect with yourself, too.

I don't know how my life would have turned out had I been able to put all this into words twenty years ago, let alone be consciously aware of any of it back then. Like with all fundamental truths in life, those insights didn't mushroom overnight. It's certainly with mixed feelings that I look back at the 20-year-old me, who had no idea that a life-long, mysteriously strong urge to dig deeper, to expose, layer by layer, the realness of real would turn into an adventurous quest heavily entangling private and professional life, walking down rocky roads through various foreign countries and cultures, financial sacrifices and debts, deep shame, brilliant education, true friendships, unmasked broken-heartedness, and never choosing the easy way out in order to not betray myself.

The love for objects with soul and personality has been around since my childhood days, but only now I've come to fully understand how we're not only connected to the people around us, to nature, to everything we feel drawn to, but also to seemingly "lifeless" objects.

So, open up, become aware, and use your eyes to see. Look deeper than you normally would and become truly aware of what you surround yourself with daily. The quality of the clothes you are wearing, what fabrics do you wrap your precious self in? Natural fibers or polyester? What material are your shoes walking you through life made of? Natural materials or plastic? Where does your coffee mug come from? Was it mass-produced anonymously for millions of people around the globe or thrown on a potter's wheel, which makes it unique? Which blankets do you tuck your kids in when you kiss them good night? Are they made from natural fibers or polyacrylic (which is based on crude oil, as is polyester)? Where do you buy your food? From supermarket chains or the local farmer's market?

When it comes to evaluating your things and their essence, also consider the (often inhumane) labor conditions and the composition of the materials used. Besides, quality standards in countries of production, if applicable at all, are rarely the same as in our home countries; therefore, you might want to spare a thought for the number of objects in your homes emitting noxious vapors due to harmful chemicals used during the production process.

It goes without saying that handcrafted objects have more essence, more life, than any mass-produced item could ever have, hence vibrating the highest. The famous quote, "Quality isn't expensive. It's priceless," fits very well here, too. Patty Aubery, who wrote the foreword to this book, once said, "Why would I put a price tag on my priceless life?" and of course she's right. We need to value ourselves more and claim back a pristine yet substantial aspect of us by reconnecting to the spark of life that lives in all of us—and in special objects, too.

Whenever you decide on quality over quantity, you also honor the company behind the product (an increase of vibration in itself). Luckily, there are still manufacturing companies out there that have never stopped believing in their craft and in their products. Many of them have stood innumerable tests of time and are still around today, while other companies of the same industry came and went, fading into history without leaving any trace.

The distinguishing factor between "gone" and "still in business," you might have already guessed it, is quality, of course. But there's more. Willingness to take risks, far-sightedness, overcoming challenges with new perspectives, keeping a balance between technique, state-of-the-art, and heart, resilience, knowing when to hold on and when to let go, a sense of heritage, and building long-term relationships with partners and clients, based on mutual trust (sounds a bit like a well-balanced recipe for a successful individual life, right?). Every single traditional company has their own set of rules or standards ensuring ongoing business success, and they might differ from each other in various ways, but what they all have in common is the uncompromising principle of top-quality, the passion for their craft, and the life-long willingness to constantly serve the best to their customers. To serve you. To pass on to you a product of their heart and soul, to share with you time-proven values, to ground you by offering you a real possibility to hold on to something solid and assist you in the expression of your authenticity. Your awareness, appreciation, and support not only keep sparkling history alive, but you also become a part of its essence.

You might be familiar with the quote, "Everyone is born unique, but most of us die a copy." As shocking and sad as this sounds, it is true. Therefore, choose uniqueness and quality in every way that feels good to you, and you'll always be your most authentic self, vibrating high.

ABOUT BARBARA LANZ

With an ever-open mind and unique out-of-the-box thinking, Barbara connects dots where others do not even see dots and encourages her surroundings to do the same.

In her late twenties, she gave up her successful international career in cultural event and conference management after realizing that her tasks often lacked substance and true meaning. She embarked on a quest for authenticity, self-improvement, and personal growth and returned to university to study political science and her childhood pet subject, art history. Eventually, she graduated with a master's degree in fine and decorative art from Sotheby's Institute of Art in London. Additional experience in logistics services, retail, real estate, and top-notch technical sciences research round off her multi-faceted fields of work, which fostered a curious, open mind, but most importantly, trained her to quickly grasp the essence of things and get right to the core no matter the complexity.

Barbara strongly believes in quality and the expression of authenticity throughout all aspects of life. She inspires her private clients to add value to their personal environments and assists traditional companies and manufacturers in introducing their products to a wider audience.

To find out more about Barbara and how you can increase your vibrations, please visit the website www.bespokevienna.com or get in touch via welcome@bespokevienna.com.

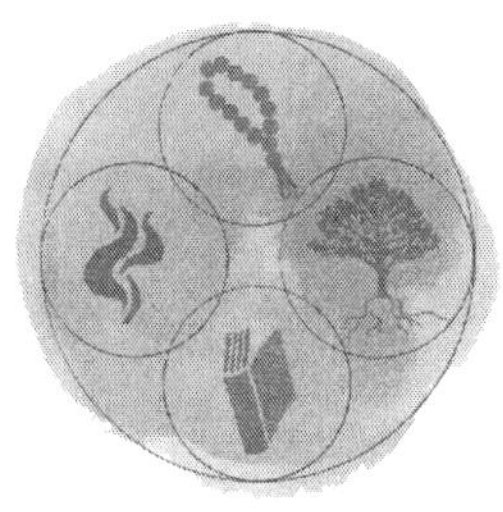

YOU ARE WORTHY!

Erin McCahill

I am not supposed to be here!

There was a moment when I thought my story would end in the dark waters of the ocean with my breath slipping away, stolen by the hands of someone I trusted and loved. In that moment suspended between life and death, something sparked deep inside me—a fragile flickering of belief. It whispered, "This isn't how your story ends. You are meant for more."

Belief. Such a small word, yet it carries a power capable of moving mountains. It is the energy that transforms despair into hope, pain into purpose, and fear into courage. It's the energy that lifts us and says, "You belong here. You are worthy. You have something beautiful to give the world." I didn't always understand its power. But belief saved me, rebuilt me, and turned every scar into strength and every door I've opened to a brighter future. My journey has not been easy, but it has shown me the power of believing in yourself and the life you deserve.

Growing up, I was instilled with values that laid the groundwork for my resilience: kindness, loyalty, hard work, responsibility, independence, compassion, and the belief that everyone has the power to create opportunities no matter their circumstances.

My parents taught me to never judge a book by its cover, to look for the good in others, and to be grateful for every day and all you have. I carried those lessons into every corner of my life, but the world doesn't always play by those rules, and I found myself tested in ways I never imagined.

As a young girl, I struggled to find my footing. High school was especially difficult after transitioning from public to private school. I wasn't prepared for the rigor or expectations. I failed English my freshman year—the very subject that demands you to express your voice. This failure rocked my confidence. But something inside me refused to give up, and I worked through summers, doubled up on classes, and clawed my way back. By the time I graduated, I turned failure into fuel.

That experience taught me a powerful lesson: *setbacks do not define us; they shape us if we let them, and it's how we rise that shows who we truly are.*

When I transitioned to college, the challenges continued. Independence brought freedom but also a steep learning curve. I stumbled, but I refused to let setbacks define me. Each failure taught me a lesson; each struggle built a layer of strength. Looking back, I see how these early battles shaped the woman I've become: determined, hopeful, and unwilling to give up.

This lesson would echo throughout my life, especially during the years when I faced far more than academic struggles. The strength I gained during those formative years became the foundation I leaned on when my world began to unravel in ways I never imagined. Throughout my life, seeds have been planted along my journey. As I look back today, there was a reason I was put in certain places at specific times: to learn a lesson for something that was going to happen in the future.

In junior high, my friends and I would assist my neighbor by serving the summer lunch she held for the battered women's association. As a freshman in high school, we catered a battered women's association meeting. I remember this day as if it were yesterday. Wearing my white top, black skirt, and red apron, standing in the kitchen with the plantation shutters open, listening to courageous women speak about their situations. I could not understand or comprehend why anyone would put themselves in a situation like they described. I turned and asked my neighbor, "Why would they not just leave if someone hit them?" and "How could someone truly lose their self-identity? No one can be brainwashed." She looked at me, and she said, "Yes, it happens."

My father had just passed away, leaving me raw with grief and in one of the most vulnerable times of my life. I remember the evening I walked by him, and he said hello. He was charming, attentive, and eager to take care of me—he seemed to be everything I needed and would become my first husband.

Believing and going after my dreams was harder to hold onto when I found myself trapped in an abusive marriage. The signs were there before we said, "I do"—the rage-filled outbursts, the controlling behaviors, the broken objects—never toward me, but I dismissed them. I was taught to see the good in others, to help, to overlook flaws. On our wedding night, he hit me. And it didn't stop there.

I endured physical and emotional abuse that stripped me of my identity. My life was threatened and became a cycle of walking on eggshells, apologizing for things I didn't do, and trying to "fix" what was unfixable. I was stunned, frozen by disbelief. I thought, "Maybe I said something wrong. Maybe I made him mad. Maybe this is my fault." I excused it, justified it, and buried my fear under layers of denial. But the abuse escalated. I felt trapped, powerless, terrified, and completely alone. There was no way I could let anyone know what was going on.

I stayed because I was afraid. Afraid of what he might do if I left. Afraid of the unknown. Afraid that maybe, somehow, this was all my fault. It's a fear so many of us carry in situations like this, a fear that whispers lies about our worth, our strength, our future.

I fell off the WaveRunner into the water and couldn't balance getting back on. He flew into a fit of rage; my husband held me underwater and attempted to drown me. I remember an out-of-body experience, a voice reminding me of my brother's advice about conserving breath underwater. I saw myself—coaching myself underwater to let the bubbles go slowly to conserve my breath. I clung to that advice, and somehow, he let me up. I gasped for air, and a lifeguard came out and pulled us back to shore. Somehow, I survived. Somehow, I escaped.

This moment changed everything. It was the clarity I needed to realize that if I stayed, I would not survive, and I remembered that young girl standing in that kitchen catering and listening to the courageous women sharing their stories. I'm so very grateful that with the help of dear friends, I left. Leaving wasn't easy. It took courage I didn't know I had and a belief I could barely hold on to, but it saved my life.

Starting over was terrifying. I moved across the country. Every step of rebuilding felt like an uphill battle. I didn't share my story with anyone for a very long time—I carried the weight of shame and silence. But slowly, brick by brick, I began to reclaim my life, my identity, and rediscover the woman I had lost during that time.

I began to create the life I wanted. I threw myself into my career and have had the most amazing experiences and some not so amazing experiences along the way. But I continued to push through, believing in myself. My father taught me how to build a brick patio and do many other projects around the house. These lessons have become metaphors in my life: resilience is built step by step, brick by brick, with patience and persistence. Believing is your vision and cannot be taken away from you. Just like a strong foundation stays solid no matter the storms or changes it faces, your deep beliefs also give a firm base for your actions and decisions. This foundation shows that your belief—your vision—is a steady, lasting support inside you that outside forces can't break down.

I remarried many years later, believing I had finally found peace and stability. But my second marriage brought new challenges. This time, the abuse wasn't physical—it was emotional and financial. I was manipulated, betrayed, and exploited by someone I thought I could trust. Once again, I found myself questioning my judgment, wondering how I could have ended up here again. When I finally discovered the truth—evidence of infidelity, deceit, and lies—I knew I couldn't stay.

The strength I'd gained from my past gave me the courage to walk away not only from this marriage but also from situations and relationships that were not healthy. Starting over yet again felt insurmountable. The fear of being alone, the fear of starting over yet again kept me in this marriage and other situations longer than I should have stayed. When I finally walked away, I felt a mix of relief and grief. I'd lost pieces of myself, but I also found something invaluable. The understanding that I am worthy of love, safety, respect, and the life I desire. I had to rebuild not just my life but my sense of worth. Belief was my anchor. I held onto the belief that I deserved better and that I could create a life of joy and purpose despite the pain.

One of the most transformative moments in my journey was when I shared my story of the struggles of navigating life and looking for a job during one of the most historic times, the COVID-19 pandemic. I shared my story with the world on *60 Minutes*. It was there that I finally realized the value of vulnerability and sharing your story. Admitting that I needed help was not a sign of weakness; it was the beginning of my empowerment. That my story can be a guide for others and spark a light in someone else and give them hope. That everyone can overcome their struggles by believing in themselves and create the life they desire. No one is alone on this journey.

One of the most profound lessons I've learned is that we are all worthy. Worthy of love. Worthy of safety. Worthy of happiness. Worthy of being here. It doesn't matter how many times life knocks us down or how deep our scars run—we are worthy of rising, of starting over, of creating the life we dream of. Paying attention to the red flags is imperative. Trust your instincts, even if it feels easier to ignore them.

If you're reading this and feel trapped, hopeless, or afraid, I want you to know that you are not alone. I've been there—in the dark, in the fear, in the silence. And I want you to know that there is a way out. It starts with one small step.

Just one!

Believe that you deserve more. Believe that you are strong enough to take the next step, no matter how small. Believe in yourself. Seek help. Reach out to someone who can guide you. You don't have to have all the answers right now. You just have to start and trust that the path will unfold.

I am living proof that it's possible. Rebuilding was not easy, but it is worth every step. I rediscovered who I was outside of the rules others had forced upon me. I embraced my values—kindness, loyalty, and hard work—I began to create a life that reflected them. I have continued to be successful in my career, travel the world as an international, TEDx, experiential speaker, and have become an international best-selling author! Yes—Me! The girl who failed freshman English and lost her self-identity along the way, a domestic violence survivor.

The seasons of life will change. The darkness will not last forever. I know how impossible it feels to imagine a better life when you're in the midst of the storm. But it's there. Brick by brick, you can build something beautiful. I was not supposed to be here—or so I thought. But I am. And I'm not just surviving—but thriving. Because I chose to believe.

We are all worthy to be here. We are all worthy of the lives we dream of. And when we believe—truly believe—that we deserve better, the universe begins to align in ways we can't always see.

You are worthy. You are enough. And you are not alone.

ABOUT ERIN MCCAHILL

Erin McCahill is a corporate leader, entrepreneur, and a personal and professional culture creator. With an extensive background in the telecom, technology, and financial industry, Erin has built a reputation for building new and revitalizing low-performing organizations that deliver exceptional results. Her strategic leadership consistently delivers superior customer and employee experiences. A Bachelor of Science in business management and an MBA complement her achievements, alongside numerous industry awards recognizing her success.

Erin's journey extends beyond the corporate world, highlighting her passion for inspiring others to overcome challenges and achieve their dreams. A three-time #1 international best-selling author, International Experiential and TEDx speaker, Erin uses her platform to share a powerful message of resilience and freedom. Having faced profound loss and survived domestic violence, she channels her experiences into actionable lessons on dreaming big and living fearlessly.

Raised in Connecticut and now residing in southern New Jersey, Erin enjoys sports, travel, entertaining, and quality time with family and friends. Erin is building her legacy and is determined to give others hope and inspire them to live the life they desire. Follow her journey through her social media channels to connect, collaborate and learn more from her.

To connect with Erin

Web: www.mccahillcollective.com
Facebook: www.facebook.com/erinamccahillmba
Instagram: @erinamccahillmba
LinkedIn: www.linkedin.com/in/erinamccahillmba
Email: erin@mccahillcollective.com

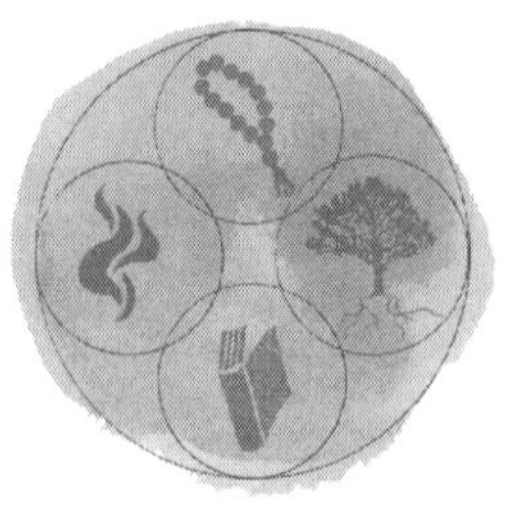

FAILURE: FROM FETAL ALCOHOL SPECTRUM DISORDER AND FAILURE TO THRIVE TO A MEANINGFUL LIFE

Ericha Scott, PhD

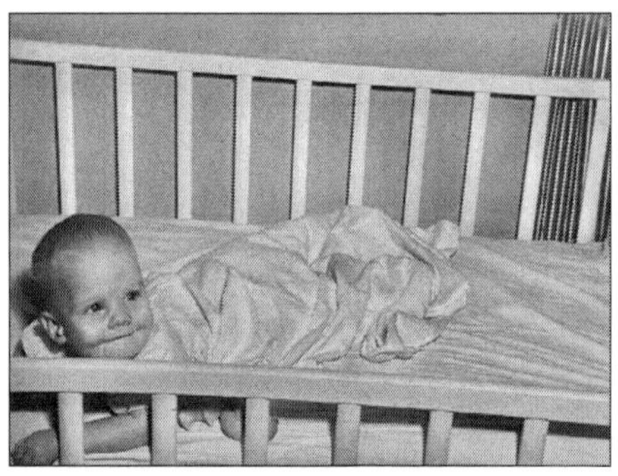

I was called "Stupid," "Slow," and "Poor Pitiful Pearl" for the first 18 years of my life. My mother was wrong to do so, but not entirely wrong. I was born with Fetal Alcohol Spectrum Disorder (FASD) and organic and non-organic Failure to Thrive (FTT).

In my mother's twisted theology, I was a failure before I was born. In her mind, it was my fault for being conceived. She was not entirely wrong there, either.

At age 13, tired of listening to how she never chose to have children, I turned to her and said, "I chose you!" Silently, Mother's eyes flew open wide in shock, and I watched as she quickly turned to walk away from me. I stood stark still, holding in my conflicted emotions. I was unsure if my statement was true, and I felt tremendous relief that her obsessive tirade had stopped. This belief, valid or not, helped me later. Believing that I had chosen her to be my mother helped me develop agency and competency in a life destined to fail.

Even though I am an expert trauma psychotherapist, I never wanted to publish my own trauma story. There are so many. I was not inspired to add my story to the mix. Even though, for many decades starting in the mid-1980s, the brave, honest, and revealing stories I heard in my office strengthened and helped heal my clients and me. This is an unpopular belief, but if the therapy is good and includes healthy professional boundaries between the therapist and client, the therapist is also healed by what is witnessed in the session. Only the most jaded person cannot help but be inspired and uplifted by watching miracles.

What opened my heart to sharing my story with the public are the impacts of a toxic exposure at work in 2005 and the long-hauler effects of COVID-19 on my aging body. These new challenges are shockingly reminiscent of my childhood experiences. So, I have been sitting with them and reflecting.

In my late sixties, I found myself dealing with a new level of cognitive and physical illness reminiscent of my childhood problems. I always knew these problems had never been completely healed, but until the toxic exposure at work and COVID-19 three times, I could not have imagined such a significant regression to early states of impairment. Then, I faced the fact that I had inadvertently kept secrets that could help heal people.

FASD, toxic exposures, and COVID-19 may all be forms of traumatic brain injury (TBI). The fact that FASD is a TBI is commonly understood. It is my opinion that oxygen deprivation during an episode of COVID-19 is also a TBI, and the virus was complicated by my previous exposure to solvents. In a way that does not appear to be scientific, doctors do not seem to want to talk about it or explore what it might mean.

According to CDC research, Fetal Alcohol Spectrum Disorders may affect as many as 1 in 20 births in the United States. This means that FASD is more common than autism. Yet, as a nation, we are behaving as if we are the dysfunctional family members of an alcoholic or drug abuser. We are living in denial, a form of unconscious lying; therefore, we cannot disclose the secrets we are keeping from ourselves. This means we are enabling an utterly preventable and tragic epidemic problem with our silence.

According to the CDC, there is no safe amount of alcohol consumption while the mother is pregnant, especially during the first trimester. Alcohol is a teratogen, a poison that has long-term (throughout the lifespan) harmful effects on the fetus and the adult human being.

The psychiatric field would have had a long list of diagnoses for my mother. Many of them would be justified. As a clinician, I think of her in these terms, and I see her as a very immature and un-evolved soul. As a human, she is my mother, which includes the full range of paradoxes of her psyche and our relationship. At one point, she was so destructive in my life that I banished her for twenty years. The final straw was not a monumental event. It was the tears of a male waiter who was serving us in a very fine restaurant as he listened to my mother emotionally berating me at the dinner table.

This story is one of chaos, serial tragedies, and many miracles. I was unplanned, unwanted, and, by the time Mother's pregnancy was discovered, impaired by her drinking. Mother told me one night, when I pressed for more information, that in 1953, she wanted either an abortion or to give me up for adoption. Both decisions would have been wise for her. Neither decision was approved by her stepfather, the patriarch who insisted she have the child (me) and arranged a marriage to make it socially acceptable.

As a young woman, Mother was a privileged, beautiful Tennessee debutante who graduated from a "fine" finishing school, Hockaday College in Dallas, Texas. After reading my mother's high school and college yearbooks, I suspect she was an alcoholic before she attended college. Not only was she drinking heavily, but she was also very argumentative with her childhood and high school friends. There are too many notes inside the yearbook cover from friends who beseeched her to resolve ongoing disputes. Later in life Mother admitted to me and others that she was an alcoholic. I never saw her sober until after she was admitted to a nursing home.

My grandmother remarried when my mother was seven. Mother was adopted by her stepfather years after they married. Family legend is that William was president of First and Peoples National Bank for forty years, then retired to Chairman of the Board for another twenty years. My grandmother's family, the Chenaults, have lived in our small town as gentleman farmers, lawyers, and city administrators for five generations.

To illustrate Mother's privilege, her wedding gown, made by nuns in a convent outside of Paris, is stored at The Henry Morrison Flagler Museum in Palm Beach. Her fall from grace would have been brutal for the most mature and stable person. It was crushing for her. She never fully recovered her emotional wellness, financial security, or social status. When Mother became pregnant she had just divorced the love of her life, an Air Force pilot who had been captured in Korea. When he returned, their marriage did not last long. Their marriage was likely challenged by Mother's inability to become pregnant, the escalation of her drinking, and his PTSD as a survivor of a Korean POW camp.

Seven or eight years later, the second marriage, an arranged, loveless, and conflicted one, also fell apart. This was not a surprise. I was six, and my half-brother was two or three. I joke about this scene, but it is not funny. I clearly remember Mother shouting, "Get in the car; we are moving!" From Dad's perspective (the man who agreed to an arranged marriage to make my mother's pregnancy respectable), he showed up for our weekend visitation to find the house empty. About the same time, I sat in the back seat on our long drive from Texas to Tennessee softly singing, "Remember the Alamo," until I was told to "Shut Up!" Throughout all of this, I was struggling with Fetal Alcohol Spectrum Disorder and Failure-to-Thrive.

While she was dying, Mother disclosed that the doctors never believed I would live until adulthood, and if I did, they did not think I would have a normal life. I did not have a normal life. At times, I had an outstanding and exemplary life, coupled with a few catastrophic failures, but it was never normal. The paradox of normal versus not normal has been a theme throughout. It may surprise you, but I would not change much of my history. There were many gifts that have been born out of my disabilities. It has taken 50 years or more to claim them as part of my blessed birthright. To claim the gifts I have been given or developed through hardship has brought moments of liberation. My wounds carry the magic I have to offer the world.

Mother told me I nearly died as a newborn. I did not find evidence to support this in my birth records. This does not mean it isn't true. I was able to confirm she had a difficult pregnancy and birth, which included a story about "falling down the stairs." I place this story in quotes because I suspect it was my mother's attempt to induce a miscarriage. Her report about labor is that the obstetrician told her to shut up and stop screaming. In a condescending way, he explained that she would not remember the birthing process. The doctor's comment was a reference about how endogenous oxytocin helps a mother forget the painful effects of childbirth. He may have counted on the prescription of Dilaudid he had administered to assist the oxytocin. Mother, in the middle of labor, said she sat straight up and screamed at the doctor, "TO HELL I WON'T REMEMBER!!!" This story, I believe. This scenario exemplifies my mother.

Some of my physical and developmental challenges were evident immediately, and others were revealed over time as I grew up. I was born with a cleft palate with no lip involvement, minor cranial facial deformities (which might be an indicator of chromosomal damage), a hearing loss, and chronic colic. The polyps on my ears were fetal gills, which are usually reabsorbed before birth. The cleft palate, which was mild but caused problems with tone and speech, prevented me from being able to suckle. Mother used a soft plastic baby bottle with an enlarged hole in the rubber nipple to feed me. Mother, from the position of a victim, described how she "had" to pinch me so I would open my mouth to scream. This enabled her to squirt baby formula into the back of my throat. Today, there is more attention to healthy maternal bonding and better suggestions for how to feed a baby unable to suckle.

I had severe colic, which can be caused by swallowing air

and the resultant painful gas. When a baby has a cleft palate, the palate is not closed properly, so air is swallowed. Colic can also be caused by an underdeveloped gastrointestinal tract, which is not an uncommon result of exposure to alcohol in the womb. In Matthew Perry's autobiography, he reveals that he had colic, and by age two months, in 1979, his mother was given a prescription of phenobarbital to help stop his crying. One of the many tragic and unsurprising revelations in his book is how he abused phenobarbital as an adult.

I am not sure if I was given phenobarbital in infancy. I do know that I was given alcohol. During a period of deep personal exploration, I had an intuitive suspicion that someone had put alcohol in my baby bottle. I asked my aunt if this was a possibility. I was prepared to respond in a neutral fashion to her denial and protest. Instead, she shocked me with, "Well, hell, I put whiskey in your baby bottle! You never stopped crying!" The problem with this type of solution, such as a barbiturate or alcohol, is that the root cause of the infant's pain is not addressed. Additionally, a baby's liver is not fully developed; therefore, it is not able to process or detox alcohol or a powerful drug.

There were a few surprises associated with long-term fetal alcohol effects, problems I had not attributed to exposure to alcohol in the womb. I suspect many people have these same problems but do not make the connections with fetal development either. As I sought to make sense of my health problems in childhood, some misattributed to other issues, I researched, wrote, and published a paper in a Southern California Licensed Marriage and Family Therapist (LMFT) newsletter on Fetal Alcohol Spectrum Disorder. Several years earlier, I was a doctoral dissertation committee member for Canadian Michael Irving, PhD, who researched pre- and perinatal art therapy. His doctoral committee included several internationally renowned pre- and perinatal medical doctors and psychologists.

My mother reported she stopped drinking around the seventh

week of my fetal development. During my research, I realized the etiology of many of my childhood, adolescent, and early adult physical problems were due to alcohol exposure as a fetus. I am confident Mother stopped drinking when she said she did. My birth weight was well within the range of normal, and my overall impairment would have been much more severe had she continued to drink.

When I was around age 20, a doctor, with little warning, stretched my urethra in a way that was exceedingly shocking and painful. He said my urethra was deformed, and it was the reason I had so many urinary tract infections. Later in life, Mayo Hospital discovered my esophagus was abnormally narrow, so much so that my doctor stood up when I walked into the room to receive the results and shouted, "WHY didn't you tell me that you can't swallow?" Calmly I said, "Because I never could. I eat soft foods, soups and ice cream." The first time a friend asked if I had had enough time to eat my dinner, after I had found myself sitting alone at the table again, tears welled up in my eyes.

Exposure to alcohol in the womb has an impact on the immune system. Therefore, I was ill throughout my childhood. I had chronic strep throat, bronchitis, and pneumonia. In addition, it took several surgeries to correct my cleft palate.

Being in and out of the hospital was normal for my early years. Since most of the cleft palate surgeries were before the age of four, my early memories of the hospital are sparse. I remember waking up in the middle of a surgery surrounded by men in white lab coats with round mirrors in front of their eyes and a bright light shining in my face. I still remember the clicking of the nurse's heels on the terrazzo floor, and due to my drugged state, they seemed to echo.

I was given so many antibiotics that my adult teeth were discolored a very dark grey. Many of my baby teeth needed to be pulled so the adult teeth would have room to emerge. This is not an uncommon problem for those with fetal alcohol effects. I can assure you this was not pleasant. As I was preparing for this book chapter, I compiled a list of the challenges associated with my birth circumstances. Even for me, it was shocking. I knew I was a miracle before making the list, but now the magnitude of this miracle felt overwhelming.

LIST OF PRIMARY AND SECONDARY FETAL ALCOHOL EFFECTS: cleft palate, mitral valve prolapse, hearing loss caused by nerve damage in utero, autoimmune problems starting at birth, multiple hospitalizations and surgeries in early childhood, minor cranial facial deformities at birth which might suggest chromosomal damage, colic and gastrointestinal problems, severe allergies, learning and processing problems, developmental delays, significantly underweight until college, chronic fatigue throughout my entire lifespan which has been exacerbated by toxic exposures and COVID-19, chemically sensitive to environmental toxins, shorter by two inches than the women in my family, deformed urethra, joint problems (wore corrective high-topped shoes in childhood), my senses (touch, taste, smell, loud noises, and light) are highly tuned in ways that are distracting (these sensitivities are commonly attributed to PTSD, but for me these challenges are primarily biological, and secondarily trauma based), and discolored teeth.

FAST FORWARD TO FOURTH GRADE: By the time I was repeating fourth grade, I had attended seven schools in three states. I was nine years old. Mother was visiting my class, and I overheard my teacher say, "You know she really likes art. Why don't you hire a private art teacher?" I remember thinking, "THAT IS A VERY GOOD IDEA!" Mother hired Jim Compton, a beatnik artist with long hair, a gold earring, a beret for a hat, worn-out jeans, and flip-flops. It was 1963, and I had never seen anyone like him before. I remember staring at him in awe. He taught me weekly private art lessons for the next 12-18 months. During that time, I passed fourth grade, and by the end of fifth grade, I was reading college-level. While my academic success was variable, my overall progress continued. I took the CLEP test (college-level examination program for advanced placement) and exempted two classes by scoring college-level in my two favorite subjects, English literature and biology. I attribute this miraculous success to the healing properties of art.

My experience as a nine- and ten-year-old is why I never doubted the ability of art to heal my clients, no matter what problems they brought to the session. Today, sixty years later, we have significant, reliable, and valid research that verifies what I have been observing for years: art's ability to help heal trauma, whether it is neurological, biological, psychological, cognitive, spiritual, or a combination. More than a few clients have said with wonderment, "Who knew art could save my life!"

A few other miraculous experiences solidified my recovery trajectory and my pathway as a wounded healer therapist. At age 30, I was at a crossroads. I had no idea what to do next. I loved my career in the art world as a museum curator for the Polk Museum of Art in Lakeland, Florida, and as a fine arts college instructor. I had taught photography for a community college and as an assistant to Jean-Pierre Cannelle for The Cleveland Institute of Art in Lacoste, France. I had my first and last one-woman art show at the Polk Museum of Art at age 25.

In 1985, I was hired, with no academic training or work experience in psychology or addiction, to provide a primary counseling group for those with substance use disorders in a 200-bed hospital. During the interview, any staff member who wanted to ask me questions was encouraged to do so for five hours. It was a grueling day. I decided to take the job for a year and see if it might be a good career fit. One day, I asked my supervisor what I should do with a difficult group. He said, "Oh, I don't know. You are an artist. Why don't you use art?" So, I did!

A few months later, my younger brother was hospitalized because he suddenly developed a stutter, and he was so dizzy that he was unable to walk without falling. During a scan, the hospital found a brain mass. When I visited him, I brought art supplies and a technique I had read in a book by Bernie Siegel, MD, entitled Love, Medicine & Miracles. I asked my brother to draw his brain mass as if it were a monster. Then, I would turn the page and ask him to draw it again but smaller until it was the size of a dot. I noticed that he was much more relaxed by the time visitation hours were over, but beyond that, I did not know what to expect. I hoped a miracle might happen, but honestly, I was doubtful. The next morning, I returned to the hospital to find my brother in the lobby, finishing up paperwork and talking to the doctors. He had been discharged. He no longer had a stutter, and he could walk normally without holding onto the furniture. His brain mass had disappeared overnight. I was elated, and at the same time, I knew I could not be confident that art had healed him. Still, I was inspired and curious. This "miracle" started me on a journey of exploration and study on the topic of creative arts therapies for the last forty years.

That same year, the executive director at work approached me to say, "We just received the results from our outcome studies, and your clients had fewer relapses than any other therapist in the hospital." I had been praying for signs from above, and between my brother's miraculous healing and this outstanding feedback, the signs appeared to be clear. As much as I loved working in the art world, I decided this was the path I was supposed to take. As of this year, I have been an employed, certified, or licensed counselor for forty years. This did not mean all was hunky dory. For most counselors, working for residential substance abuse programs can be outrageously stressful due to low pay, daily crises, and extremely long hours.

To illustrate my point, during that first year as a residential counselor, my immune system collapsed. I began living on antibiotics again, just as I had in childhood, as if these drugs were daily vitamins. Fortunately, I mentioned this to a sober woman at a social gathering. She was a lab technician for a hospital, and she was wonderful and ruthless. Responding to her challenges, I felt as if she was intervening upon a drug addict in denial, and I was full of resistance. I could hear myself arguing with her. I could not imagine functioning in the world without the aid of antibiotics. I asked her, "How will I be able to work?" She said, "I don't know, but you have to find another way."

She explained that I was taking one of the strongest antibiotics on the market, and if I became very ill, there would not be an antibiotic able to help me. She was wise and did not pretend to have an answer, yet she was insistent I had to change. It took me about a year to find a solution, but thankfully, I found a medical doctor homeopathist. His remedies worked, and I was able to wean myself off antibiotics. Since then, I have been able to go years at a time and even a few decades without any antibiotics. When I can afford it, and often even when I cannot, alternative and integrative medicine has been my first resort. It was important for my success to find nontraditional and traditional ways to heal my body.

As a trauma expert, I would be remiss if I did not point out that the trauma, grief, and loss I experienced growing up functioned as an amplifier for my physical birth defects. Fortunately, art and creativity helped with those problems as well. Not only did I paint, I wrote a lot of bad poetry. It did not matter if the poetry or art was good or not; it helped me.

Growing up, I repeatedly advocated for myself and my brother, even when I had no hope it would make a difference. The only people who stood up for us were our black housekeepers. Every single housekeeper placed their jobs, income, and safety at risk to protect us. I have a deep love and respect for Laura in Dallas, Augusta in Tennessee, and Eloise in Florida. These three women taught me love, integrity, and courage. There was one other person who tried to help, Reverend Cochran, who was our youth minister in Florida. Unfortunately, my mother responded to his inquiry about what was happening at home by moving out of state.

I was able to reconnect with my mother in a healthy way about twenty-five years ago. I set firm limits and boundaries before I allowed her to visit me and my now-deceased husband. I had requested that we avoid hot topics during our first face-to-face visit in twenty years. She could not help herself and said with indignation, "I just don't believe spanking is abuse!" I surprised her by expressing my agreement. I said, "Mother, this is why I do not call what you did spanking." Then calmly, I listed her childrearing actions that were unacceptable. Her eyes became wide, and I found myself leaning away from her. Then she managed to calm herself and say, "That was done to me, and I did it to you, and I am sorry."

The last thing my mother said to me before she died was, "I just love you bunches and bunches, can't you feel it?" I could. In my opinion, this is another miracle.

Sheer grit helped me change my life. It also helped me trust my intuition and what I loved, such as reading, art, writing, poetry, photography, traveling, public speaking, and my career.

Throughout my healing trajectory, there were large blocks of time when I allowed myself to feel uncomfortable as I changed my worldview and ways of coping. For example, I forced myself to participate in social groups until I finally began to enjoy them. Since that time, I have participated in a wide variety of creative, spiritual, political, and professional support groups.

Since I had no reliable family, I knew I needed community. I have been blessed with an extensive collection of beloved friends and a surrogate family since I was 19, primarily the Naxon family in Dallas, Texas. Even with their wonderful help, I know how people suffer in silence, and therefore, I speak up for disempowered and oppressed groups.

Since the 1980s, I have spoken up for victims of childhood trauma, child prostitution and child sex trade, those who engage in profound self-mutilation (my published doctoral research), and victims of extreme, organized, and ritualized trauma and torture. I also speak about the healing nature of art and how, when practiced by a well-educated and certified art therapist, it is highly effective.

After much searching and exploration, I developed a dedicated spiritual practice of prayer and meditation. I became a certified interfaith spiritual director. My love of nature has always been and always will be a great source of comfort, spiritual connection, and beauty.

These are the keys to my healing: 1) facing uncomfortable personal and family truths, 2) taking accountability for what was set in front of me, sometimes even when it was not my fault, 3) setting good boundaries for as long as I needed, 4) reaching out to heal the familial rifts when I was strong enough to do it safely and well, 5) finding effective alternatives to my complicated health challenges, 6) trusting my intuition and wisdom over the reductionistic health mythologies of our times, 7) using art and all creative processes for personal enjoyment and physical, emotional, and spiritual healing, 8) spending time in nature, holy sites, and traveling to foreign lands, 9) never giving up even when I wanted to do so, 10) forgiving those who had repeatedly caused me grave harm and ultimately—more than that—loving them unconditionally.

If this path of self-exploration interests you, I hope you will call me at 310-880-9761. I offer creative arts intensives in my office from 1 to 10 days. I will be honored to walk by your side as you heal your past, present, and future.

ABOUT ERICHA SCOTT, PHD, LPCC917, ATR-BC, REAT

Dr. Scott has been a healer who has walked the fine line between mysticism and evidenced-based psychotherapy for forty years. She is a licensed clinical professional counselor (LPCC917), interfaith spiritual director, Reiki master, and a dually certified creative and expressive arts therapist. She is a published poet, artist, international best-selling author, and keynote speaker.

Dr. Scott is an honorary fellow for the oldest trauma organization in the world, The International Society for the Study of Trauma and Dissociation, and is an expert in grief, trauma, dissociation, self-harm, nightmares, integrative health, and the creative arts psychotherapies.

She has designed and facilitated art psychoeducational and creative arts therapeutic workshops for four decades. She has been recognized throughout the United States and abroad for her original, unique, and powerful healing experiences.

Dr. Scott's clinical writing and academic research have been published in trade magazines, textbooks, and peer review journals by *The Journal of Chemical Dependency*, UCLA, Oxford University Press, and Taylor and Francis.

To learn more, please visit her website at www.artspeaksoutloud.org. To book her for an individual creative arts intensive in Malibu, as a worldwide group retreat leader, a keynote speaker, or as a consultant, please get in touch with her directly at 310-880-9761.

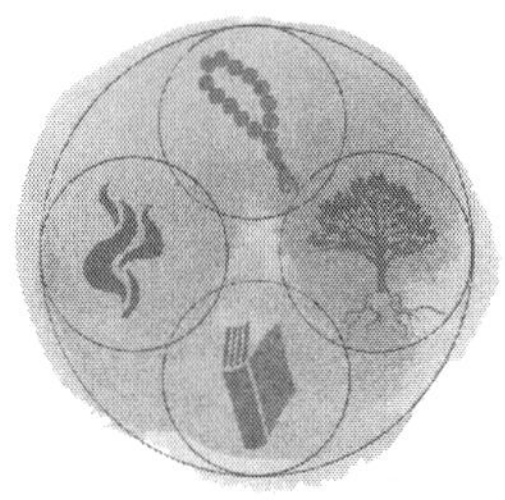

CHOICES AND CHANGE

Candice Shepard

Here's the thing about change. Even when it's the right move, the thing you wanted, the shift you planned for and prepared for and worked for, it can still be so hard. You wanted this change and made proactive steps to accomplish it, but what happens when you get what you prayed for and find out it's still difficult?

I don't make decisions lightly. I plan and prepare and work my tail off for everything I want. And I've handed every piece of my life over to the Lord from a young age. But I have not always done so willingly or peacefully. I can be stubborn and bullheaded, and when I set my mind to something I have a tendency to put my head down and plow forward no matter what. That's sort of a double edged sword. It's a fantastic trait have when you need to persevere through tough times, but when you need to move in a different direction that trait can cause unnecessary pain and delay.

I went through some pretty significant and difficult life circumstances in my early teen years, ones that precipitated life evaluations when most girls are thinking about boys and parties and college. I had those same focuses, but they were marked with a heaviness, a weight that was unusual for someone of my age and stage in life. I found myself, at the age of 15, full of despondence in the presence, fear of the future, a certainty that I could never have the life I wanted, and therefore contemplating unhealthy ways out. In my immaturity I didn't see a lot of good options. I cried out to the Lord in my anguish and heard the voice of the Holy Spirit tell me to hang on, heard Him tell me that everything I was going through would result in good things. So, I hung on.

I threw myself into every good thing I could find, everywhere I felt I had a gift, or potentially had a gift, that could be cultivated. I learned and read everything I could get my hands on. I participated in music and theater and athletics of all kinds. Challenge myself academically? You bet! Join the Army at the age of 17? Sure! Move across the country, hate it and come home again? Attend a top 20 law school? Be a courtroom litigator when I was one of those humans who would rather face death than public speaking? OK!! Not a fantastic plan, in hindsight, but it all worked out. I worked hard, found my ability to believe and dream, and left the past in the past.

I decided to become an attorney, not so much because that was a specific dream of mine, but because I felt an urge to do something big and important in the world. As a Communications major in college I learned the art of speaking and writing in a lot of different venues and situations. As a student in Law School I learned that my brain was a massive asset that could be trained to do whatever needed to be done to accomplish anything I wanted to accomplish. As a practicing lawyer, I did a lot of things, but the thing I was most proud of was the ability to help people who found themselves in really hard places. I built a life I loved.

Over the next 30 years I achieved things that, on paper, are pretty impressive. I am humble enough to know that all of my accomplishments are gifts from God, but also confident enough to know that because I am obedient and worked hard and used the gifts He gave and continued on with an unwavering belief despite circumstances that would make many quit, we made it happen. I've had the opportunity to do some really amazing things.

In 2015, I was led to open a law firm. Radical honesty, I did not want to do that at all. It felt like a lot of work that I wasn't sure I was up for. I had 3 young children and a 4th on the way from an orphanage in Ukraine. A start-up of any kind is challenging, but a law firm that relies on me to know things and do things and hire and manage people is a lot of a challenge. I argued with God for many weeks about it. "I don't want to do this, please don't make me do this."

My shiny new business plan said we'd lose money for the first 12-18 months, but God had other plans. We broke even in month one, were profitable by month 2, and a multi-million-dollar producer by year two. We purposely built a law firm that was unlike most law firms. One in which client comfort and care was as important as the work itself, where Jesus showed up in every corner, and where we had the hard conversations in order to have the best outcomes. We have had the opportunity to serve and help thousands of people with very difficult matters, with a smile and compassion, and often with prayer. I am grateful to say that I am part of a lot of stories of overcoming, of beginning again, of finding belief and healing and joy. It's such a privilege.

We expanded quickly. I threw every piece of me into that firm, gave my all for my clients and my staff. Then things started to shift again. I didn't fully know it at the time, and didn't understand it, but I was being led to completely start over. Again. And when I say completely, I mean 100% brand new nothing looks the same as it did in 2015. I could feel the change coming, like a north wind that blows through town and rustles all the leaves. Change was coming and I didn't like it.

My 15 year old self and everything I had gone through, still buried deep inside my adult soul, underneath all the accomplishments and the pain of the past that hadn't yet been fully healed, started whispering. The whispers became a nudge. Then the whispers and the nudges became more and more insistent such that I could no longer pretend they weren't there. The time had come to use all of that hardship, all of that pain, all the overcoming and the believing beyond myself and my limited sight and abilities, all of the preparation I had done over the previous 30 years and do something completely new and different.

So I prepared for this new thing. It required the use of all the skills and knowledge I had gained, along with a new set of skills and knowledge. So I worked. I healed. I learned and I grew. And as I was being led to do something new, and worked on the preparation, my stubbornness again said "I don't want to do this, please don't make me do this."

And so, in my stubbornness, some of the decisions and planning were taken from me.

People and relationships and business and opportunities and finances and so many things that I took joy and pride in started being stripped away. I cried a lot of tears and cried out in anguish yet again, feeling alone and abandoned and betrayed. Wondering why all this is happening to me, feeling sorry for myself and searching for ways to keep what I had.

But God, in His infinite wisdom and kindness, had plans. I had gained enough wisdom to understand that His ways are better than my ways, and He was leading me toward the answers to prayers that were for the good of all, not just Candice. It was beautiful and hard and tragic and amazing. Honestly, if I wasn't so stinking stubborn I probably wouldn't need to go through all the tears, but here we are. Finally, I gave in to the reality of the new thing. I surrendered to the God of the universe who was calling to the little girl inside me to dream again, to use what had been prepared in me over the last 35+ years.

Here I am north of 50 starting something new. I'll come back to that in a moment, but let's first acknowledge that starting something new means ending something else. The end of something, no matter what the circumstances, requires a letting go, a making peace, a grieving of what was in order to make way for what is and can be. It is beautiful and hard and tragic and amazing. And even though I know that I know that I know that this is the path God has put me on for a very specific and important reason, I have grieved the end of that thing I created. That thing made sense. The legal career and the law firm I created from nothing came with financial security and gravitas and a certain amount of credibility. That law firm was safe. There were people I loved to work with and work for. There was predictability and comfort. And now I am stepping away from it in order to reach out toward something new.

There are a million analogies about this, but perhaps my favorite is the visual of rock climbing, something I will admittedly and unashamedly never ever do in real life, but I love the visual. When you're climbing up the side of a mountain there are parts of the climb that are smooth and easy, and parts that are treacherous and scary. There nearly always comes a time when you have to let go of a great hold in order to reach up for the next hold, knowing that for a moment in time you'll be without an anchor, suspended in space, launching upward toward the next great hold, risking a total freefall but believing that you'll soon be anchored in an even better place. But also knowing that if you don't let go and surge forward you will never reach the place you're supposed to go next.

So, here I am, north of 50, starting something new, letting go of a really good hold in order to surge upward to the next place, a dream that has no certainty but a lot of potential for greatness. I've been called to believe in something that makes little sense to me and no sense to a lot of people who have always known me as "that lawyer." Yes, the dream I had been pursuing and accomplishing was a big deal but it's ok to have another big dream. The dream I'm letting go of, the accomplishments I'm laying to rest, still matter. But because the something new is a God-sized dream, I am willing to release the old dream for a new one.

The new dream is an amazing adventure! We have created a

new business with a new business model: Aurora Network, the only all-female Christian life coaching company on the planet. I have truly seen nothing else like it.

From an early age, many of us are told to make ourselves smaller, be quieter, don't rock the boat, help others be comfortable, do what is expected of you. But that's not what God created you for. Women are magical, created by Him to be so. There is magic in you. And that little girl quietly waiting for you to listen to the whispers and the nudges to go live out your God-sized dream, needs you to believe that.

Aurora Network was created to encourage that. We have created a platform for coaches who want to do the creative work without having to do the business "stuff" and who want to do the work alongside other like-minded women. We have also created spaces for women who need support and help and hope and healing as well as a nudge to listen to the nudge telling her to dream again.

Aurora is all of us collectively believing beyond ourselves and our human understanding. It's a community of believers, stepping out in faith, believing that the hardships we have endured will not be in vain; that God will make beauty from those ashes; that by simply believing in the God of the universe and his promises, rather than relying on our own understanding, we can use all of the lessons we have learned over the years and all the tears we have shed and create a life that is nothing short of extraordinary.

Believing that every time we have had to let go of something we wanted (or thought we wanted), or something we thought was the best we could do, or lost something we never wanted to let go of, it was to walk toward God's very best. The fact that we can do all of that in community with one another is a gift.

When we lock arms with other women, when we refuse to let the belief and the faith and the love in us fade, even though that might make sense in the moment, we can change the entire world. For the good of the Kingdom. For the eternity we have been promised. For the life and the eternity He has for you.

That 15 year old little girl who was so badly hurt that she didn't want to exist any more needs me to do this. So even though I must let go of the anchor I was holding on to in order to reach out toward something bigger than myself, I'm going to trust that the potential freefall will actually be a thrust upward, toward something even better. Together the women of Aurora Network are in battle for the souls of the universe. Women are warriors, hand knit for a unique purpose and mission. I am a warrior. You are too. I really hope you'll join us, me and the other beautiful souls of Aurora. Lock arms with us, darling girl, and we will change the world.

ABOUT CANDICE SHEPARD

From Business Success to Kingdom Purpose: Meet Candice Shepard. As the co- founder and CEO of Aurora Network, Candice Shepard stands at the intersection of faith, leadership, and transformational coaching. A certified success coach, accomplished author, and dynamic speaker, Candice has dedicated her life to empowering Christian women to step boldly into their God-given purpose. Under Candice's leadership, Aurora Network has become a beacon of hope and excellence in the Christian coaching community.

Drawing from her extensive experience and deep faith, Candice has created a supportive ecosystem where female Christian coaches thrive and where clients facing any number of situations find the perfect blend of spiritual guidance and personal growth.

Ready to Transform Your Journey? For Potential Clients:

Are you a woman seeking to align your business success with your spiritual walk? Join our community of purpose-driven entrepreneurs who are experiencing breakthrough results through faith-based coaching. Book your transformational session with Candice today and discover how to elevate your excellence while deepening your faith. Aurora also has coaches who specialize in other areas ready and willing to work with you on your next big breakthrough.

For Aspiring Coaches:

Feel called to impact lives through Christian coaching? Aurora Network offers you more than just a platform—we offer a purpose-driven community, comprehensive training, and generous compensation. Join us in our mission to transform lives through Christ-centered coaching. Connect with Candice and the Aurora Network family today to begin your journey of purpose, prosperity, and spiritual growth. Your breakthrough awaits! www.AuroraNetwork.life

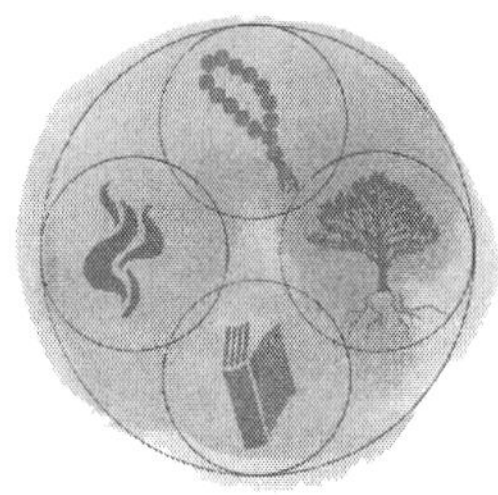

NEVER CREATE A BLUEPRINT IN INK

Jessica Skop

Thirty years ago, I had the blueprint imprinted in my head. Get good grades, go to a good college, study a major that will provide a career that brings stability (salary, benefits, 401(k), and PTO). Graduate and start my career. Get married and start a family. Work my way up in the company, retire at the appropriate age, and use my retirement accounts to live off of. That was the game of life.

I failed the blueprint.

See, at a young age, I had a fire in me that wasn't going to be put out. I didn't allow others to influence my MIND. My decisions, sometimes, but my overall mindset of where I wanted to go, well, that was mine!

I did the first part. Got good grades and went to Michigan State University. But where I shifted was, I knew being a business owner was in my heart. So, I believed beyond and created my own blueprint, with a few bumps thrown in there by fate.

I was in the corporate restaurant business with a degree in Hospitality Business and a desire to prove myself. I quickly rose through the ranks and went from manager in training to a new restaurant opener to district marketing manager of Chicago, all in under two years. I learned as much as I could, yet I still wanted off the blueprint. I wanted something deeper. I kept returning to owning my own business. Have you ever found yourself in your car on a longer trip and acting out what you would do if you owned your own business? I mean, like physically "pretending" to interview your first applicant while driving and envisioning what that would look like if you owned your own business? This girl did, 100%! Hell, I even acted out my ribbon-cutting speech and how that would feel. It was stuff like THAT, that kept me dreaming beyond what others thought possible. Fun fact, my first business, my first day spa, was an old auto parts store in the middle of a bedroom community with about 7,000 people. No joke, people thought I was crazy, and yet, it later rose to millions in sales and is now a staple in the community and surrounding areas, but more about that later.

Over the next 20 years, I lived and breathed so many things with that spa business that others would not think was possible.

Newly single mom opening a business and raising an 8-month-old on her own? Check!

Opening a business that I actually had NO experience in except from a customer service perspective? Check!

Building a team and getting them to trust in a 27-year-old to operate, manage, and lead a business? Check!

Surviving a block-wide fire that burnt down my whole business two years in? Check!

Renovating a space and re-opening 10 days after the fire? Check!

Having a contractor go bankrupt after taking the insurance payout and having to build it all again with no money? Check!

Opening a second location while rebuilding after a fire? Check! Check!

But as I went through some of the TOUGHEST times of my life, God did show me that my own blueprint was the right path. I began seeing some beautiful triumphs that just solidified my faith in what I was doing. I was being nominated and winning many business awards (over 30 in total), being featured in magazines and podcasts, joined exclusive Masterminds, met the love of my life through a sales call (been married since 2011), increased sales for over two decades in a row and so much more!

I literally went from broke and living in a 300-square-foot motel room with a new baby to the owner of a multi-million-dollar company with a beautiful family that brings so much joy. All because I believed beyond what was possible and got away from that expected blueprint. I was able to take MY dream and my scribbled, unique, designed by-and-for-me blueprint and turn that into reality. I was very fulfilled…until I wasn't.

Wait, wait, I know what you are going to say. Why on earth would I be so unfulfilled with a life of love, family, success, and being able to design what my life looked like? It was because I was complete with the spa business (day to day) part of my life. It no longer lit me up to see sales rise or to see a new promotion come to life. The day-to-day no longer served me, and in fact, the more I was in it, the more I felt trapped. It was not enough for me anymore. That fire inside me was not being fueled. Don't get me wrong, I still love the spa and our team, more today than I ever have, but something was off. And in order for our spa and team to succeed, I needed to be honest with myself.

I wanted more. More life, more experience, more joy, more uniquenes and purpose in what I did, more time with my family, and more of God's world. I felt I needed to start designing again. Start REALLY looking at what is possible if nothing was impossible. So, I started to believe again. I started to dream again and REALLY dig deep as to what I wanted and how I could make it happen.

See, I feel that the world today provides the most unique opportunities that we could have ever been given. There is a way that ANY hobby or love can be turned into a career! Enjoy knitting? Teach classes and open a pop-up! Have a gamer in the family? You can play your games online, and others will pay you for your knowledge! (I now know this from experience.) So, here's where it gets good for me. I get to open that magical catalog from the universe and start choosing what I like. And after decades of living my dream, it's time to start a new one. So, despite others not believing or approving of what I was doing (I was deviating from the blueprint again), I thought about what lights me up.

It brings joy to my heart when I am able to help other spa owners solve their marketing blocks or design. I love building campaigns and ideas for them. I've always said, "I love taking something ugly or worn down and making it beautiful!" Might be why I love flipping homes so much. I love restoring or creating beauty where it was once lost. The same can be said for marketing ideas and plans, layouts of spas, or even a mindset. On top of that, I have a desire to help women DREAM again. Be grateful again. I have the desire to create retreats that uplift and inspire women to start living a life they love and desire. I love Vision Board planning with others and opening that space in someone's heart that was closed by society and "opinions" of others. So, I created JSkop Coaching, which is a coaching website centered around spa marketing and personal mindset.

Now, my days are filled with a few new conversations behind the wheel. I now work on how I can help other spa owners build a unique marketing plan while also maintaining a mindset of gratitude for what they have. I role-play my coursework and conversations with other owners who have brought pain points to me. I am in service to other entrepreneurs who need someone who understands them. I am in the process of designing unique and uplifting women's retreats to help them restore from stress or open their hearts to new beginnings.

My days are also filled with dreaming alongside my husband. We are probably the most diverse and unique in "what do you do for a living" type couples around. See, my husband and I started a real estate business during the pandemic where we flipped homes and then started investing in rental properties. That got my juices flowing with the concept of owning Airbnbs and how I could create beautiful women's retreats at those Airbnbs. My husband and I keep creating revenue streams that light us up, that keep us believing beyond what is possible. Hardly anything we do is normal or mainstream. And yet, it keeps growing and opening more doors. It has provided us time with each other, time with our sons, travel, and so much more.

So, my final advice to you is grab your paper and PENCIL and take some reflection time to build your own blueprint. Is it truly yours? Does it need to be adjusted? There is so much magic in this world that you need to grab ahold of that and create the blueprint that fits YOU. What the rest of the world thinks of you is not your business. God and his universe has an open book of options. Which one will you start with? Just be sure to never create your blueprint in ink. Good luck and God bless!

ABOUT JESSICA SKOP

Jessica Skop opened Serendipity Wellness Spas in September of 2004 in Linden, MI. After a devastating fire in 2007, she reopened 10 days later and expanded from a 1,200 to a 6,500-square-foot 2-story full-service spa and wine café while adding another location in Frankenmuth, MI.

Jessica worked with mentors/companies such as Inspiring Champions, WhizBang Training, Ritz Carlton Training, Jack Canfield, Tony Robbins, Dean Graziosi, Kate Butler, and Chet Holmes.

Jessica has won several awards: Woman Owned Business of the Year, Outstanding Customer Service Award, Entrepreneur of the Year, Enterprise of the Year, and Talk of Town 5 Star Award every year since 2010. Jessica was featured in Spa Inc. Magazine, Spark & Ignite Your Marketing podcast, TNG Worldwide magazine, and has been a two-time keynote speaker for Girls in Business.

After building her businesses into seven figures, Jessica is now coaching other spa owners on marketing and mindset and adding women's retreats. Jessica is a mother to two boys, Nathan and Hawk, and a loving wife to Ryan.

If you feel that fire that propels you to make some changes and want to talk about it, you may reach Jessica at jskop@serendipitydayspas.com or www.jessicaskop.com.

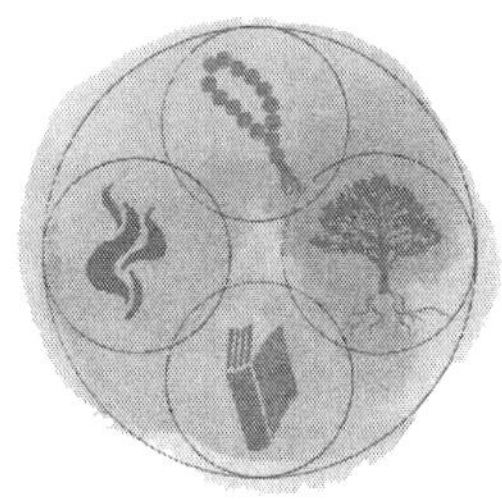

FROM LOSS TO LOVE: BREAKING THE CHAINS OF FEAR

Karen Smith

I was only eight years old when the world as I knew it crumbled beneath me. My mother—the woman who had been my entire universe, my protector, my guiding light—was suddenly gone. After a long and painful illness, cancer claimed her, leaving me feeling completely untethered and drowning in a sea of grief and bewilderment. The devastation was unlike anything my young mind could comprehend. That moment marked the end of my childhood innocence and the beginning of a lifelong struggle with fear.

Losing my mother left a deep, unshakable void that cast a dark, all-consuming shadow over the rest of my childhood. From that moment, fear became my constant companion. Persistent sense of impending doom followed me in every waking moment, causing me to cling to friendships and family members. This fear took root in my soul, chipping away at my sense of security. I developed an overwhelming fear of abandonment, haunted by the idea that I could lose anyone else I loved without warning. The world became an unpredictable and dangerous place, a minefield of unseen threats that could steal away those dearest to me without reason. For years, I lived with a gnawing anxiety that simmered beneath the surface of everything I did. As a child and into adulthood, I endured physical symptoms—constant stomach pain, a racing heartbeat, and sweaty palms. Any slight deviation in plans or a loved one's health would send me into a panic, convinced that the worst possible outcome was inevitable. The pain of losing my mother left me feeling as though there was nothing left to look forward to, casting a shadow over my sense of hope and anticipation for the future. This anxiety followed me into adulthood, becoming a defining feature of how I approached relationships, especially with those I loved most.

When I became a mother, the stakes felt even higher. How could I protect my children from harm or death? How could I protect myself, minimizing the possibility of leaving my children behind like my mother had left me? The thought of my children experiencing the same kind of devastating loss I had endured was unbearable. That fear led me down a path of overprotection and control.

In those early years of parenting, I was consumed by the desire to protect my children, to shield them from any potential harm or heartache. I believed that by keeping them close, monitoring their every move, and intervening at the first sign of trouble, I could prevent them from experiencing the pain I knew all too well. Looking back, I now realize that my parenting approach was heavily influenced by my own unresolved trauma, but also took their ability to learn and fend for themselves. What I thought was love and care was, in many ways, driven by fear.

I became a helicopter parent, constantly hovering over my children, never allowing them the space to make their own choices or take risks. Early on, I established strict rules—no fighting, no hitting, no wrestling—to avoid any situation that might lead to harm. Every mistake they made felt like a personal failure—whether it was a poor grade, being disciplined at school, or receiving a speeding ticket. I responded with harsh discipline, convinced that any misstep on their part reflected my shortcomings as a mother. This belief led me to think that fear and control would keep them safe.

My voice, often raised in frustration, became a tool I relied on, believing that through volume and anger, I could maintain control. I convinced myself that if I could intimidate them into obedience, they would remain out of harm's way. But in truth, I was only pushing them further away from me. Changes needed to be made.

The journey toward self-awareness wasn't easy. It was riddled with moments of doubt, guilt, and regret. But it was also filled with profound realizations. One of the hardest lessons I learned was the importance of consistency in providing my children with a stable and secure environment. The constant upheaval in their lives—moving from Iowa to Washington to care for my dying sister, then back to Iowa to start a new life with my husband—had left my children feeling destabilized. Their sense of security was shaken by each move, each major change, and I hadn't realized how deeply it affected them.

Children thrive on consistency. They need to feel that no matter what challenges arise in the outside world, their home is a place of stability and safety. In reflecting on my own upbringing, I now realize how the experiences of my childhood made it difficult for me to provide that same stability. Growing up with a father who, as a single parent, wasn't as present as he needed to be led to deep insecurities in my relationships—including my own children. Each time I uprooted our lives, I was unknowingly searching for something—perhaps a sense of control or the hope that a new environment would ease the pain I carried. In doing so, I inadvertently passed on that instability to my children.

There were countless moments where I overreacted—where my fear-driven parenting led to tears and tension that could have been avoided. I remember one incident with my eldest son that still haunts me to this day. He had lied about leaving his brother home alone, and when I found out, I was furious. I wasn't just angry about the lie itself; I was terrified that this small failure could be a precursor to a lifetime of mistakes and that he would somehow spiral into a life of regret and loss. In my fear, I lashed out, yelling and imposing harsh consequences without truly understanding his fear of disappointing me. That moment drove a wedge between us, one that took years to mend. What I didn't see then was that my reaction had more to do with my unresolved pain and fear of losing him than his mistake.

My well-intentioned parenting methods only created a household ruled by fear and stifling control. My children, frequently afraid of making mistakes, grew hesitant to express their true thoughts and feelings. They learned to keep their heads down to avoid my wrath, and as they got older, they pushed back against the confines I had set, rebelling in search of the freedom and autonomy I had denied them. My attempts to protect them had, in fact, driven them away. I had confused control with care, and my children were the ones who suffered because of it.

This was perhaps one of the hardest lessons I had to learn as a mother. In trying to prevent my children from experiencing pain, I had robbed them of the opportunity to grow and develop their own sense of self. Mistakes are an essential part of life—they teach resilience, problem-solving, and self-awareness. By trying to micromanage every aspect of their lives, I was denying them the very experiences they needed to become strong, capable individuals.

I remember a particular conversation with my youngest son, who was in his teenage years at the time. He had gone to a party with friends, yet when he came home, he was sullen. My initial reaction was one of sheer panic—what had happened to him? What if he had been hurt or worse? The fear was overwhelming, and my first instinct was to excessively question him until I got the answer that satisfied me. But as I stood there, about to unleash my anger, I saw the look in his eyes—one of frustration, sadness and deep hurt. In that moment, I realized that my reaction was once again driven by fear. I wasn't angry because he was withdrawn and not talking; I was terrified of losing him and having him make mistakes based on wanting to fit in with his peer group that would affect the rest of his life. Over time, I began to realize the damage I was doing. The older my children grew, the more they resisted my attempts to control them. They began making decisions behind my back, seeking the freedom I had denied them. Each act of rebellion felt like a personal failure, but with every instance, I was forced to confront the reality that I could not shield them from life's challenges. They needed to experience the world for themselves, make their own mistakes, and learn from them.

For the first time, I took a step back. Instead of lashing out, I sat down with him and listened. I listened to his frustrations, his need for independence, and his resentment toward the constant control I imposed on him. It was a difficult conversation—one where I had to confront my own shortcomings as a parent. But it was also a turning point. For the first time, I began to understand that letting go of control didn't mean I was failing as a parent. It meant I was giving my children the space to grow.

As the years went by, I began to make a conscious effort to shift my parenting approach. I started to trust my children more, to give them the space they needed to make their own decisions, even if those decisions led to mistakes. I began to understand that my role as a parent wasn't to prevent them from falling but to be there to support them when they did. I had to learn to let go—not of my love for them, but of my need to control every aspect of their lives.

This shift in perspective was transformative, both for me and for my children. The more I let go of control, the more I saw them flourish. They became more confident, more willing to take risks, and more open with me about their lives. Our relationship deepened in ways I never thought possible. Instead of fearing their independence, I began to celebrate it. I realized that the greatest gift I could give them was the freedom to be themselves, to make their own choices, and to learn from their own experiences.

Exploring the underlying reasons for my parenting choices revealed a multitude of valuable insights and deeper understanding. I came to understand the significant challenges of becoming a parent while I was still so young. At just 20 years old, I lacked the emotional maturity and life experience necessary to offer my children the nurturing guidance they needed. The absence of my own mother during those formative years only deepened my sense of inadequacy. The weight of my insecurities, coupled with my fear of failure as a parent, undoubtedly contributed to the struggles we faced as a family. As I reflect on the many years that have passed, I am filled with profound gratitude for the hard-earned lessons life has offered. I have come to deeply value the importance of allowing my children to stumble, to fall, and to learn from their mistakes. Through this, I've discovered that true communication isn't about raising your voice—it's about speaking calmly, listening with empathy, and fostering an atmosphere of trust and mutual respect. My relationships with my sons now stand as a testament to the healing power of patience and understanding. They remind me that even when the path ahead feels uncertain and we don't always have the right answers, love and resilience can guide us through the darkest times toward a future brighter than we could have imagined.

I've learned that there is no such thing as a perfect parent or a perfect child. Expecting perfection from ourselves or our children sets us up for inevitable heartache when mistakes happen—as they surely will. Granting myself and my children the grace to accept flaws, embrace imperfections, and trust that we all have each other's best interests at heart has brought us closer together. It's in these moments of grace that we discover true strength.

Most importantly, I have learned to release the suffocating grip of fear—fear of loss, fear of the unknown. Life is unpredictable, and change is constant. By embracing that uncertainty and accepting that I cannot control everything—or everyone—I have found a deeper sense of peace. I now live more fully, unburdened by fear, knowing that loss, while painful, is not the end but simply a part of the journey. In this realization, I've found a new sense of freedom, not just for myself but for my children as well.

Reflecting on my years raising children, I've come to realize that the journey wasn't just about their growth—it was about mine as well. Each challenge, misstep, and heartache became a profound lesson in love, patience, and the power of letting go. Motherhood has been a deeply transformative experience, teaching me how to release fear and embrace love fully.

It is my hope that others, too, can find value in the program that helped me transcend fear and live FEARLESSLY. To live fearlessly is to:

Have faith that things will work out.

Show empathy to others who are struggling.

Embark on a life of adventure.

Respect each other, even during difficult conversations and trying times.

Respond with love, no matter the situation.

Approach life with enthusiasm.

Take time for serenity—find your inner peace.

Draw strength from even the toughest moments.

Seek laughter every day.

And most importantly, say YES to opportunities outside your comfort zone.

As an author, coach, and speaker, my mission is to restore joy and hope to families navigating life challenges. I aim to empower them to overcome their fears, create a clear path forward, and embrace the beautiful journey of parenthood and childhood with ease, grace, and resilience.

ABOUT DR. KAREN SMITH

Dr. Karen Smith, Founder of the Living FEARLESSLY Program.

With over two decades of experience in health and wellness, Dr. Karen Smith is dedicated to helping individuals break through emotional and physical barriers to live empowered, authentic lives. Through her signature Living FEARLESSLY Program, she leads clients on a journey of healing from deep-rooted fears, past traumas, and recurring patterns that prevent personal growth. Combining her expertise in NeuroEmotional Technique, EVOX, and holistic health practices, Dr. Smith provides transformative tools to address the underlying causes of emotional and physical challenges.

Her mission is to inspire her clients to embrace emotional freedom, overcome obstacles, and create a fearless life of fulfillment and balance.

To learn more or get in touch with Dr. Karen Smith, visit www.drkarensmithdc.com or email her at healingheartsandbodies@gmail.com.

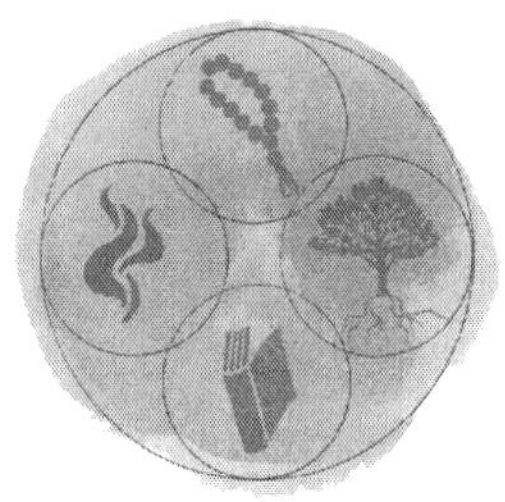

LIVING BEYOND LIMITS: HOW TO HAVE IT ALL

MiShawn Williams

There are moments in life that strike with such clarity that they forever shape you and light your way. Sometimes, these moments come unexpectedly—during an ordinary drive, at a simple stoplight, or while taking a familiar turn. They arrive like whispers from the universe, telling us that everything we've wanted or believed in is already within reach.

For me, two such moments happened—both in the car. They were more than just realizations; they were revelations that would shape my entire life philosophy and, ultimately, my purpose. These moments weren't just about me—they held a truth that I knew others could embrace, a truth that could unlock abundance and fulfillment in anyone's life.

Eight years ago, I sat at a stoplight, but as I waited for the light to change, an extraordinary wave of awareness washed over me. Suddenly, I was profoundly present—more present than I'd ever felt. I looked around and I saw my life, not just in pieces, but as a whole, vibrant mosaic.

The style of home I lived in was what I had envisioned over a decade ago. I had real estate investments, a loving partner, a beautiful child, and my own business. Each of these elements had once been a dream, a distant "what if," but now, they were my reality. My heart swelled with deep, resonant gratitude. It hit me: I wasn't just living a good life—I was living the exact life I had imagined. I realized, in that moment, that everything I had ever wanted was already here.

Then, a thought struck me. **If I could create this life, so could anyone else.**

That's when "having a life of having it all" became crystal clear. "Having it all" isn't a myth or a privilege reserved for the lucky few. It's not the outdated image of a perfect balance between family, career, and status. No, our "All" is deeply personal. It's the life we imagine when we let go of limiting beliefs and an either/or approach to life. It's about knowing what you want and believing that it's possible.

Your "All" is already within you.

The Power of Belief and Visualization

I always knew I wanted to be a mother. I remember when I was ten years old, walking home from the mall. Out of nowhere, I heard myself think, "I want to be a mom one day." It felt so real, so certain, that the memory stayed with me for decades. But knowing what you want and believing it's possible are two different things, especially when life presents challenges you didn't expect.

Thirty years later, I was sitting in my OB/GYN office, listening to the nurse practitioner explain my hormone levels. She spoke kindly, but her words carried an undertone of concern. She ended with, "You know, I was adopted, and it was great." I walked out feeling dizzy, struggling to process what she had really said. The message was clear: the journey ahead wouldn't be easy and was unlikely.

I was 40 years old, just beginning my pregnancy journey. Of course, I knew it would be challenging. But knowing the facts and feeling the fear didn't stop me from believing. Even when the path was filled with obstacles—failed IUDs, multiple IVF attempts, a miscarriage—I held on to that belief. I *had to.*

Scared. Anxious. Restrained. On edge.

Those feelings were real, but so was my vision. I used visualization and affirmation like lifelines. Every day, I imagined my future child in my arms. I saw it, felt it, lived it in my mind. Visualization wasn't just wishful thinking; it was an active practice. It meant seeing the outcome as if it were already here—feeling the joy, hearing the laughter, singing the lullabies. Affirmations reinforced that vision, grounding me in the belief that what I desired was not only possible but inevitable.

Visualization and affirmation together became my anchor. They didn't erase the fear or the setbacks, but they carried me through them.

After multiple failed attempts, countless tears, and endless prayers, it finally happened. With the third IVF cycle, at the age of 44, I gave birth to the most beautiful baby boy. Holding him in my arms for the first time, I knew—this moment was the manifestation of every visualization, every whispered affirmation, every faithful action, every ounce of belief I had fought to hold on to.

Age was just one constraint I had to move beyond.

Breaking Free from Limiting Constructs

We all carry invisible boundaries—beliefs handed down through generations, absorbed from society, or woven into our identities so subtly that we don't even notice them. These constructs shape what we think is possible, often keeping us small, contained within a version of life that doesn't reflect our true desires or authentic selves. I learned this firsthand when I came out to my father.

I was 18, nervous but resolute, a Daddy's girl about to share a truth that felt both liberating and terrifying: "Dad, I'm bisexual." I loved my father deeply, and his opinion mattered to me more than I could express. His reaction was a mix of concern and confusion, colored by his own limiting beliefs. He said things like, "Our family members won't want you around their kids," words that hurt. But beneath his fear, there was also love. He wanted to understand, even if it meant facing his own discomfort.

He agreed to attend a PFLAG meeting with me—a space for families and friends of the LGBTQ+ community to learn and support one another. I hoped it would help him see me more clearly. Once there, we split into small groups, parents and children sharing their experiences. My father opened up about my coming out, his voice filled with vulnerability. Someone in the group said something that shocked me: "Oh, she's really gay. She's just going through her bisexual 'stage.' I just want you to be prepared."

I was horrified. How could a stranger presume to know who I was? In that moment, I realized something profound: We are all living within constructs—expectations, judgments, and narratives—that limit our full expression. They exist everywhere, in every community, and they shape not just how others see us but how we see ourselves.

These invisible boundaries can prevent us from accessing our "Have It All" life. They keep us trapped and disconnected from our true desires. To break free, we have to start by noticing our disempowering self-talk.

How do you catch your own limited thinking?

Start by paying attention to fear, especially fear that revolves around a lack of something. Notice any self-talk that sounds like:

- "I don't know enough."
- "I don't have enough."
- "What if I can't do it?"
- "If I do this, I can't have that."

Once you catch those thoughts, ask yourself: "Is this really true? **How do I know this?" Challenge your narrative.**

Your true, abundant life lies beyond these constructs. When you identify and release them, you open space for new possibilities. You step into a life where you are fully self-expressed, aligned with your deepest desires, and free to create the reality you want.

Abundance and Financial Freedom

For many of us, financial security feels like the ultimate marker of success. We want to know that our bills are covered, that we can take care of our families, and maybe even enjoy a few luxuries. But money, more than anything else, often triggers our deepest fears and limitations. It's easy to fall into a mindset of lack, telling ourselves, "I can't afford that," or "That's too expensive." I've been there, too.

I remember the first time I saw the price of the new car I wanted. My immediate reaction was, "What?! How will I afford that?" The same thing happened when I considered attending my first personal development retreat or investing in a five-figure program. Each time, the voice of lack whispered doubts: "You don't have enough. You're not ready."

But then, something inside me shifted. I paused, took a breath, and listened to my intuition. Instead of focusing on what I lacked, I tuned into the energy of abundance. I reminded myself, **"I am always provided for. Things always work out."**

It wasn't about denying reality or ignoring financial responsibility. It was about changing my relationship with money—from fear to trust. When I made those investments in myself, they felt risky, sometimes even reckless. But each one opened doors I couldn't have imagined. The car helped me up level my life. The retreat expanded my mind. The program transformed my business.

Abundance isn't about having unlimited financial resources; it's about knowing you are always supported. When you shift from scarcity to abundance, money becomes less of a stress and more of an energy you attract. The things you once thought were out of reach become accessible, not because the numbers changed but because your mindset did.

This shift isn't just about money—it's about how you see the world. When you release the fear of lack, you open yourself to possibilities. You start to notice opportunities you once overlooked. You trust that the resources you need will come, often in unexpected ways.

Gratitude: The Gateway to "All"

Abundance is already here.

Abundance isn't something you chase; it's something you tune into. It's not a distant future or a set of external achievements. It's here, now, woven into the fabric of your everyday life. The roof over your head, the food on your table, the love in your life—all of these are expressions of abundance. But the key to unlocking its full potential is gratitude.

Gratitude amplifies abundance, turning what you have into enough and then more than enough.

Gratitude isn't just a fleeting emotion; it's a practice, a way of seeing the world. When you focus on what you have, rather than what you lack, you shift your energy, and you become keenly aware of the treasures that surround you.

I remember making the turn into my neighborhood that day and feeling an overwhelming sense of gratitude. It wasn't just a surface-level "thank you"—it was deep, resonant, almost aching. I felt grateful for everything: the car I was driving, the palm tree lined street I was on, the home waiting for me, the beautiful child I had fought so hard to bring into the world. Every detail felt like a gift.

Gratitude turns the ordinary into the extraordinary. It transforms what you have into enough and then more than enough. When you're deeply grateful, you're not focused on what's missing; *you're immersed in what's present.* And that presence opens the door to wealth . . . a wealth of what's possible.

Think about it: When you're in a state of lack, you're closed off, defensive, fearful. Your energy contracts. But gratitude is expansive. It opens you up, *softens you*, makes you receptive.

Start where you are. Take a moment, right now, to look around you. What can you be grateful for? Maybe it's the chair you're sitting on, the device you're reading this on, the quiet moment you've carved out for yourself. Maybe it's the people who've supported you, the challenges that have shaped you, the dreams that still light you up.

The more you practice gratitude, the more you'll see. It's like tuning a radio to a new frequency. At first, you might only catch glimpses of the signal. But the more you practice, the clearer it becomes. You start to notice abundance everywhere—in the small things, the everyday miracles.

Gratitude amplifies abundance. When you focus on the good, you create momentum. You start to expect good things, and those expectations shape your reality. It's not magic; it's alignment. When you're aligned with gratitude, you're aligned with abundance.

Living Your "Have It All" Life Now

We often think of our dreams as something far off, waiting for us in the future. We say, "I'll be happy when I have the perfect partner," or "I'll feel successful when I reach that six-figure income." But the truth is, your "Have It All" life isn't out there somewhere—it's here, now, waiting to be seen and felt.

The key is presence. When you're fully present, you're not chasing a future version of happiness. You're grounded in the richness of this moment, where abundance already exists. It's easy to overlook the gifts in our lives when we're focused on what's missing. But when you pause, take a breath, and really *see* what's around you, you realize that you are already living parts of your dream.

Your life, right now, holds everything you need to access abundance. The relationships, the experiences, even the challenges—they're all part of your "All." When you tune into gratitude and presence, you're not just noticing what you have; you're fully experiencing it.

Take a moment to reflect:

- What parts of your life are already aligned with your vision?
- How can you deepen your appreciation for them?
- What small moments bring you joy that you might be overlooking?

Presence turns ordinary moments into extraordinary ones. That simple cup of coffee in the morning becomes a ritual of self-care. The time spent with loved ones becomes a celebration. Even the challenges you face become opportunities for growth and transformation.

I experienced this again when we made the decision to move to Mexico with my husband and young son. The idea felt exhilarating but terrifying. As a parent, I had so many fears about the unknown—Would it be safe? Would he adjust? Was this the "right" thing to do? I realized how much I was still locked into constraints about what was "permissible" as a parent. These fears were just another set of invisible boundaries, whispering limits that weren't real.

But I took the leap. And on the other side of that fear, I found incredible joy and adventure. Our lives expanded in ways I couldn't have imagined. We discovered new cultures, made new friends, and shared experiences that enriched us. It was a reminder that beyond every fear lies a world of possibilities waiting to be explored.

Your "Have It All" life isn't a destination; it's a way of being. It's about showing up fully, appreciating what's here, and trusting that more is on its way. When you live from that place, you don't just wait for abundance—you create it.

Embracing Purpose

Every moment of clarity, every challenge overcome, and every leap into the unknown has shaped not just my life but my purpose. That second defining moment in the car was in declaring my life purpose. It was a culmination of every experience, every realization, and every piece of wisdom I had gathered along the way. My purpose became clear: **to inspire and empower others to be fully self-expressed and to have a life of "Having It All."**

This isn't just my story; it's a universal truth. Abundance, purpose, and full self-expression are available to everyone. I believe that when you pursue your purpose, you walk hand-in-hand with something greater—Universe, Source, or Infinite Energy—I call it God. It's a path illuminated by trust and filled with gifts.

Your purpose is your compass. It guides you through the fear, the unknown, and the challenges. When you align with it, you tap into a source of strength and clarity that transcends circumstance.

I've seen this in my own journey, and I've seen it in the lives of others. The moment you step into your purpose, something shifts. The fears that once held you back lose their power. The limitations that seemed insurmountable begin to dissolve. What remains is your true, beautiful, relentless, joyous, unbounded soul—ready to create, expand, and move.

Your "Have It All" life is not a dream—it's a possibility waiting to be claimed. It requires curiosity to explore, creativity to envision, and courage to receive. It's about knowing what you want, believing it's possible, and taking inspired action, even when the path is uncertain.

Wherever you are, know that you're standing at the doorstep of endless possibilities. This isn't just my story—it's a reflection of what's possible for you too. Your "Have It All" life isn't a distant dream; it's a thrilling adventure that begins with a single step.

I invite you to step into the life you've imagined—the one that's already waiting for you.

- Know what you want and **dream boldly.** What does your "All" look like? Let your imagination direct it!
- **Believe with your whole heart,** even when the path feels uncertain.
- **Break free and dance beyond limits.** Challenge those old stories that try to restrain you.
- **Celebrate what you already have.** Gratitude is a practice where abundance grows!
- **Take inspired action.** Move forward with excitement, knowing the universe is cheering you on.

Your journey is yours to create, and every step is a chance to discover new joys and parts of yourself. Fear might show up but remember: beyond that fear is a world full of wonder waiting for you. When you take that leap, you'll find life unfolding in ways more beautiful and exciting than you ever imagined.

You are limitless. Your dreams matter, your purpose is real, and abundance is already flowing through your life. So, take that leap. Your "Have It All" life is here—not someday, but *right now.*

Embrace it!

ABOUT MISHAWN WILLIAMS

MiShawn is a speaker, coach, and facilitator. Her style is "elegant empowerment" and she loves to guide people to discover their unique brilliance and create lives worth celebrating.

A Certified Jack Canfield Success Principles Trainer, former Self-Expression & Leadership Program Leader, Life Purpose Coach, and Fascinate Certified Advisor, MiShawn has led numerous personal development and leadership programs. She is the founder and host of the expert interview series "The Emerging Entrepreneur Show." MiShawn also brings a holistic approach to transformation as a Certified Chakradance Facilitator, guiding clients to transcend limitations through movement.

With a passion for wine, MiShawn is a Founding Wine Ambassador with the Boisset Collection, an international wine company, and leads a multi-million-dollar team of wine enthusiasts. A contributor to the #1 Amazon Best Seller *Moms Who Boss Up Post-Pandemic*, MiShawn is also a wife and proud mom to an adventurous 8-year-old.

Through workshops, retreats, or keynote talks, MiShawn delivers a blend of wisdom, encouragement, and inspiration that leaves people lit up and empowered to take joyous, bold, transformative action.

MiShawn is happy to connect with you for speaking, coaching, or on the socials.

https://linktr.ee/MiShawn
MiShawnWilliams.com

Cheers!

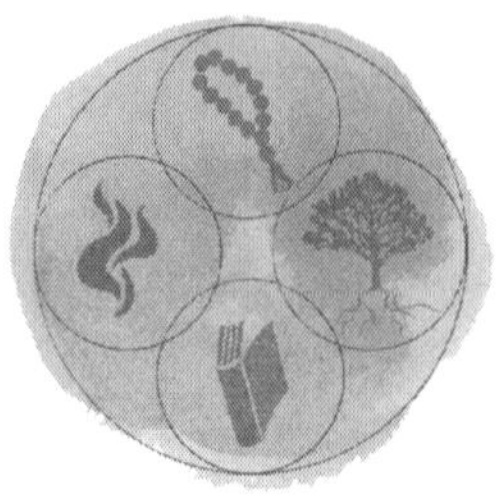

POWER OF AUTHENTICITY

Christina Giannone

There's a moment when you realize you've lost pieces of yourself along the way. For me, this chapter of my life has been about healing—about blossoming back into who I used to be, only better. It's a process of letting go of the survival armor I didn't even know I was wearing and reclaiming the parts of myself I thought were gone forever.

In my twenties, I didn't understand the effects of trauma. Back then, we didn't have endless resources making mental health a mainstream topic. So I trudged along, believing I was confident and self-assured, all the while seeking validation from everyone around me. I wanted everyone to be happy, to approve of me. But looking back, I can see how trauma peeked through the cracks in my self-image.

Over time, I started noticing things I was tolerating that the old me would have never accepted. I'd ask myself, *Why am I putting up with this?* It was a jarring realization: I'd let my boundaries dissolve. My intention now is to rebuild them and return to the unapologetic version of myself—the one who wasn't afraid to stand firm. But this time, I want to do it with grace, not armor.

When I was younger, people found me intimidating. That

always puzzled me because I thought of myself as kind and giving. But I was also fiercely outspoken and direct. I see now that this was a shield I wore, shaped by my early experiences. It was survival, a way to navigate the world after a turbulent start in life.

I was adopted at five years old, but not as an infant. I knew I was adopted, and I remembered the life I had before. I lived with my biological uncle and aunt in Costa Rica before being removed. My brother and I were found living in a car for a week, just two and four years old. It was chaos, but my uncle didn't want us to leave the country. He fought to keep us in Costa Rica, even knowing he couldn't care for us.

The adoption process was harsh and difficult. It took three years. To my uncle, I was stolen. To my adoptive family, I was saved. And to me? I didn't know what to feel. I was too young to understand what was happening, but the scars were already forming.

My biological mother was just a child herself when she had us. Thirteen when she gave birth to my brother, fifteen when she had me. She kept my brother for two years but didn't want me. My uncle agreed to take me only if she gave him my brother too. She kept all her other children but gave me away. Why? I've asked myself that question my entire life. Was it circumstance?

Something about me? I'll never know.

I think the hardest part of this journey for me was losing the relationship with the only biological sibling I have here. He has a different perspective and that is his journey to take. I chose to take this journey of healing because I didn't like the person I was becoming. Loving yourself

means taking a deep look into aligning who you are and who you want to become.

I grew up knowing I was different—not just because of my ethnicity or adoption but because of my unwillingness to conform to any facades. From an early age, I saw through the cracks in the

polished picture of our lives. I felt like my adoptive mom

strived to create an image of a perfect nuclear family, but I couldn't ignore the dissonance between what we portrayed and what my experience was.

These traits of being outgoing and blunt made me the "black sheep" and the scapegoat of the family. If something didn't sit right with me, I called it out. Hypocrisy? I'd point it out. Unfairness? I'd challenge it. My mother's response was often emotional withdrawal or silence—sometimes for days—to teach me a lesson about compliance. It didn't feel like love; it felt like control.

By the time I was eight, I fully grasped the complexity of my reality. I realized I was never going to fit into the mold she had crafted for me, and I didn't want to. My identity as a proud Latina was a point of contention. There was a false narrative that we were Italian and Irish—a fabrication my mom encouraged to avoid about our true heritage—I rebelled. I told anyone who would listen that we were from Costa Rica, that I was Latina, and that my heritage was beautiful and worth celebrating. I felt like my mom would not celebrate this part of my life, and this part of me felt like an attempt to erase *me* entirely.

Even as I grew older, the dynamics didn't change. My relationship with my mom felt conditional. She often reminded me of the "gift" she had given me by adopting me, framing it as if I should be forever grateful for being "saved" from my circumstances. I came to my own decision that love wasn't love if it came with strings attached. I felt like I was only acceptable if I stayed within the acceptable lines of someone else's vision and standards.

My authenticity was important to me, critical even, for my growth and getting to know and love my true essence. I was just trying to live my truth.

In recent years, I've embraced who I am more than ever. I've surrounded myself with people who celebrate my authenticity, who don't ask me to hide parts of myself to make them comfortable. I've learned to find validation within, rather than seeking it from others.

My message to anyone who has felt like they don't belong—whether in their family, community, or the world—is this: be who you are. Don't change yourself to fit into someone else's idea of who you should be. The right people will love you for you. The ones who don't? Let them go. Living authentically is worth the price of letting go of relationships that ask you to compromise your truth.

For years, I was told I should be grateful. But I've realized that my gratitude isn't for the life I was given—it's for the strength I found to stand tall in the face of rejection and adversity. I'm grateful for the journey that taught me to believe in myself. And I'm grateful for the realization that, no matter how broken a story begins, we all have the power to rewrite it.

Growing up in this tangled web of abandonment and dysfunction shaped me into the black sheep, the scapegoat. I was the one who spoke out, who questioned hypocrisy, who refused to stay silent. It made me strong, but it also made me wary. I built walls, mistaking them for boundaries, and wore defiance like a badge of honor.

Now, I'm dismantling that armor. I'm learning to be strong without being hard, open without being vulnerable to harm. This healing journey isn't about going backward. It's about moving forward into a version of myself that's kinder, both to others and to me. I'm reclaiming my voice, not to shout but to speak with intention. I'm embracing the fullness of my story, the messy and the miraculous.

Healing isn't linear, and it isn't easy. But it's worth it. Because underneath the layers of pain and protection lies the essence of who I am—a person who is worthy of love, belonging, and joy. This is my intention: to blossom back to me.

I believe beyond the pain of the past. I believe in the power of authenticity. And I believe that being true to yourself is the greatest gift you can give the world.

To further connect with Christina, you can reach her at:

cigiannone@yahoo.com

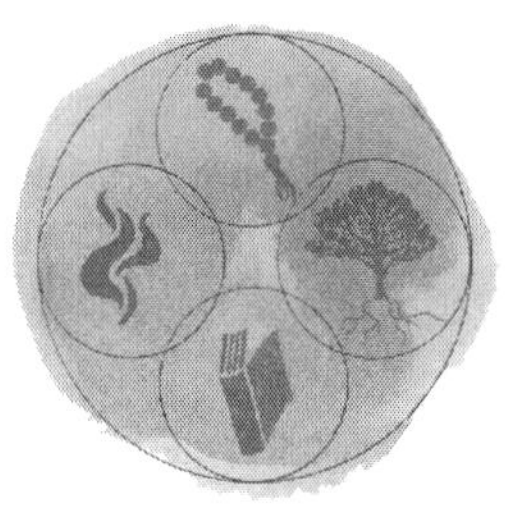

SEE THE POSSIBLE

Andrea Gutmann

Let's embark on a journey together, one that weaves together themes of resilience, perseverance, hope, and inspiration. Walk alongside me as I share the story of my middle daughter, Aria, who, at just eight years old, has faced more challenges than most could imagine. Yet she continues to pave a way forward where we are encouraged to see what is possible if we look past limitations and consider a more inclusive world where everyone can thrive.

When we enter parenthood, we often carry a vision of who we want to be as parents, of how we'll raise our children and guide them toward being better versions of ourselves. We swear we'll do things differently from how we were raised, convinced we know what's ahead. I was no different. But, like so many mothers, I was surprised to find that the journey unfolded in ways I never expected. Though I had spent years around kids as an educator and leader, I had no idea how much my own journey would reshape my understanding of community and inclusion. I can still remember the moment I stepped into the classroom and knew, without a doubt, that teaching was where I was meant to be. Influencing and shaping the next generation felt like my purpose. From the start of my teaching career, I aimed to be the kind of educator who truly *saw* all of my students. I prided myself on my ability to connect with them, and even now, I'm still in touch with some of the students from my very first year teaching second grade. As I moved through various roles in education, I found myself drawn to inclusive practices, supporting students with diverse needs and helping those who struggled the most. It became a source of pride to be a champion for all students, to bring communities together and ensure that every voice was heard.

But nothing could have prepared me for the day I became a mother to a child who would challenge everything I thought I knew about inclusion, advocacy, and resilience. Aria, who is diagnosed with a rare genetic condition called PACS1, would become the ultimate test of everything I'd championed in my career. Suddenly, navigating the world of rare diagnoses was no longer something I was observing from the sidelines; it was a path I was walking, facing the uncertainty and emotional turmoil that comes with it. As we walk through this story, I invite you to join me in exploring the complexities of love, resilience, and the unwavering belief that every voice matters, especially the ones we hold closest to our hearts.

Our oldest daughter, Alexis, entered the world in 2010, and our journey as parents began. As parents, my husband and I navigated the parenting world full steam ahead, and Alexis ticked along with her development. Of course after a couple of years passed, we decided to embark on trying to bring a second child into the family. Little did we know this would be a 5-year journey. The short story of it all, we ventured down the road of hormones, surgery, and lots of emotional ups and downs. Following my surgery to unblock one of my tubes, we decided to take a break from the fertility drugs and just reset. Apparently, that was just what we needed, along with a trip to the Dominican, to receive the news we were expecting our second child. The excitement in our home and for our family was overwhelming! But at 32 weeks, some unexpected news arrived. Following the ultrasound, we discovered that I had a 2-vessel cord (2VC). Now, like most people in the connected world, I turned to Google for information. Word of advice, never turn to Google when pregnant! The list of potential risks included heart defects and genetic abnormalities. The uncertainty was overwhelming, but I remember telling my mom when she asked, "How are you coping?" My response was simple: "Does it matter? This child is coming, and we will love her and figure it out."

On Dec. 17, with no drama or fuss, we headed to the hospital at 6 am for our scheduled C-section. For anyone who has experienced a planned C-section, it is an odd feeling to have everything feel so routine. When Alexis arrived, it was quite the story with my water breaking in the truck, calling my mom crying, and then Alexis arriving in the later evening hours via emergency C-section. With Aria, we settled into a room, waited for doctors to arrive, and we were back in our room with a new baby by 10 am. No muss, no fuss. Now, of course inside, I was praying from the moment we stepped into the hospital, we would get no unexpected news about our new baby. After all the Google searches, I wasn't sure what to expect but was hoping the "no news is good news" philosophy would apply. Well, she arrived, and the first words from the professionals in the room were that she was beautiful, healthy, and had a lot of hair! The sigh of relief in that moment is something I cannot describe in words, but you could see it in my husband's eyes as well.

Aria was an angel. She nursed right away, was settled into a 3-hour schedule in no time, and the nurses even commented that I needed to make her cry because the new mom next door was starting to think it was unfair. Of course there was still this nagging voice inside, wondering if we were missing anything since she was a 2VC. I judged where her ears were placed on her head. Were her ears too low? Is that normal? I checked her palm crease and toes. All things I had read were markers for genetic abnormalities. I don't know why I asked these questions, as I knew it didn't matter; she was part of our lives, but I think seeking answers is a natural instinct. When Aria was a couple weeks old, our family was settled into a nice routine with Alexis in kindergarten and myself working on my master's courses during nap time. We made it to Day 27, when things took an unexpected turn.

The day that will be etched in my memory for a lifetime. As much as I wish I was "Supermom," I couldn't prevent what happened to Aria. This was the path we were meant to walk as parents, and it is the path Aria was meant to follow. At 27 days old, after a normal morning, Aria experienced a frightening episode of twitching, gasping for air, and turning pale after a feeding. I knew something was terribly wrong and rushed her to the emergency room, where a pediatrician quickly identified the signs of a seizure. The video I had taken of the episode proved to be crucial in getting us to the Stollery Children's Hospital Neonatal Unit (NICU), where Aria was taken by a neonatal ambulance just hours later.

There we sat with worry and fear consuming us in the NICU. In this particular unit, there are only 18 beds for infants, as they are all for the most complex cases. The emotional roller coaster of this place goes beyond the worry for your own child and taps into sympathy and empathy for those parents around you facing unknown challenges as well. In the NICU, you look at each other with comfort, compassion, and true empathy. I felt surrounded by a different sort of love in our time there.

By day three in the NICU, Aria had undergone an EEG, MRI, and several tests. The MRI revealed immature myelination, which is common in infants, and a heart murmur. Despite the "seizure-like" episode caught on video, Aria showed no further symptoms or seizures in the NICU. The pediatrician suspected reflux and started treatment, though Aria remained seizure-free.

On the fourth day, Aria was able to come off monitors and, to the delight of everyone, was taking tours of the unit. All the time, she was content and happy. Since she was off monitors, we were able to take her to our room in the evening. But it was then we heard the gasp for breath and scream from Aria. We returned to the unit, and following the next feeding, it occurred again. Still not as severe as before, no twitching or eye movement. The doctor ordered her back on monitors, and a short while after, while we were back in our room, Aria had a seizure, which caused her DSAT to be quite low. This was not good. She was immediately loaded with phenobarbital to stop the seizures. The empathetic look of the mom across the way was clear. We were not friends; we barely talked, but we shared the same feelings as mothers. By day five, we had the results of her EEG, which were normal, and Aria stayed seizure-free with medication. We finally went home with instructions for blood work and medication administration. Aria's medication was difficult to give and came with side effects, but it was a choice between controlling seizures or not.

Ok, take a collective breath right here. It's ok. You might be wondering how we were handling all of this and how Aria was coping coming into the next months of her first year. She truly handled everything in stride, and I swear if it wasn't for Aria, I wouldn't have handled it. But this adventure definitely tests the strength of family and relationships. Stress shows character and emphasizes how important the team you build around you matters. After a few weeks at home, things seemed to settle. Then, during a family visit, Aria developed a fever and was diagnosed with a urinary tract infection (UTI), and after more tests, we learned Aria had kidney reflux, requiring daily antibiotics to prevent future infections.

Thankfully, as time moved forward, the medical scares and emergency room trips dwindled and the next parts of our story shifted. For Aria, things were less dramatic, but for this mom, we faced a new set of challenges navigating the words of delay, milestones, normal, and disability. Follow-ups and appointments included the pediatrician, physical therapist, occupational therapist, dietician, and nurses, lasting for about 3 hours each time. These appointments could be shattering to the soul and a constant reminder of what was wrong with Aria. But when I changed my lens, I realized Aria gave me the greatest gift in shifting where I once felt sympathy for what parents go through with their children now turned to empathy. It was the ability to say, "It's ok, I know." A simple gift that changes a tough meeting or conversation in an instant in my line of work. The ability to walk in someone else's shoes and comfort them that they are not alone. Aria strengthened this passion, and right here in the story, I started to think perhaps it isn't my fault after all and maybe it really was "meant to be!"

By Aria's second birthday, she still wasn't standing or moving about and words were nonexistent. She needed a stent put in her heart because the murmur persisted and now needed ear tubes to help drain fluid. Thankfully, these ended up being routine procedures with no complications to follow, except Aria completely hates her ears being cleaned or touched. As we continued to chart our path forward and towards preschool, Aria still hadn't become mobile or had the ability to talk. She received her first set of AFOs (ankle-foot orthoses) for her ankles and legs to help strengthen her ability to stand and hopefully walk one day. And yes, if you are a Forrest Gump fan, we do call them her "magic legs."

We were definitely on the money with how unique Aria really is when we finally received the call to go for genetic testing. If you dig past Aria's chromosomes right down to the exon, Aria has a slight difference. Currently, just over 300 people have the same diagnosis of PACS1 Syndrome. It's a lot to absorb learning your child officially has a complex diagnosis, but in the end, it felt like validation. They only started researching this syndrome in 2012, joining us to a new community and once again validating that we are leaders and will continue to knock down barriers. A diagnosis, any diagnosis, doesn't need to be scary or limiting. If we shift our mindset, it can be a powerful tool to open doors and conversations.

Aria stepped into the school setting bold and ready to learn. No matter how her brain interprets the world, she feels joy and happiness with her whole heart. Aria received a walker alongside her leg braces to help with her mobility, and this was when the COVID-19 pandemic started. Aria wasn't always the easiest to motivate to move, given she was so content all the time, but one place she loved was the hockey rink. With our oldest daughter in hockey plus two additional hockey billets living in our house each year, we discovered the rink was Aria's happy place. Perhaps it was the fact that nothing traumatic happened for Aria here or it was the many fist bumps, high fives, and cheers of encouragement she received as she made her way around the rink. One thing was certain, the community loved watching Aria grow and navigate the world the best way she could. When everyone emerged to the first hockey game, post-pandemic, Aria was walking independently. There were cheers, tears, and looks of amazement for our girl. This accomplishment wasn't just hers but everyone who encouraged her and us as parents along the way. We shared it together.

The word normal holds a different meaning, I think, for our home now with Aria, as every time we tried to find "normal" another challenge was sent our way. What was key for our family at this time was the importance of finding our calm as a family in the daily routines of life in our home. The advice I would offer, from our experiences at this time, would be to simply be brave. As a mother, it would have been easy to become hypersensitive and protective of a young infant who experienced so much chaos. It would have been easy to fall into a pattern where we stayed home and worried about the "what ifs" of catching a cold or even worse, causing yet another medical distress situation. Instead, we chose to be brave and carry on with the life we envisioned our family enjoying. Each time we stepped out of the door was another success under our belts. We gained confidence as a family and with Aria.

Most days, we walk forward with hope, pride, and excitement for Aria's potential. But every once in a while, it creeps in: the reality of how hard being Aria's mom can be. To constantly advocate and explain, to say her name in a group because she has few words, and to look at fellow parents and see their "I feel sorry for you" look. It creeps in. One such story was our journey to our local pool, where we were able to start swimming lessons with our youngest, Adalyn, and Aria. Back-to-back lessons and lots of excitement. Addy was bold and brave, going through all of her lessons overachieving and yelling "AGAIN." Then it was Aria's turn.

First off, registration is this cutthroat online process where lessons fill quickly. You need to be at the ready on your computer to click on the button to get your kid in! However, I can only register Aria with her age group, and if wanting a different placement, I need to call in. Barrier number 1. But Aria should be with kids her own age, shouldn't she? I am a strong advocate for inclusive settings, but that work is hard. Why should she be with peers? Peer models are the best teachers for Aria. We witness this in her school setting. The example they set is far more impactful than what the teacher says in the classroom. Aria takes cues from those around her, and although her words are behind, she wants to keep up. So, we registered with her age group and luckily found a spot. The first lesson we started with sitting and waiting for our instructor, who was a wonderful and engaging young man. Aria knows to sit against the wall and wait. First, the kids are asked to share their name and favorite animal or food. As Aria's turn is near, of course being nonverbal, I speak for her. Right here is where it begins to creep in exactly how hard the next 30 minutes will be. We take a walk, get life jackets, and walk into the pool. All the kids take off, and I look around to see the other participants happily floating and no parents needing to hang on. Aria, on the other hand, is a spider monkey stuck to me. It creeps in a little more, especially as I can see the look on the instructor's face as he wonders exactly how this will go. Now, I find myself trying to adapt each exercise and build some confidence for Aria. When the other moms look at me, I can feel it, but I also know that many don't really "get it." They want to help but don't always know how. Inclusion is messy and hard work. The instructor adapted his lesson a bit and included a piece in the shallower end where the kids can kick their legs and then gather the rings/toys under the water while blowing bubbles and putting their faces in the water. We adapted this for Aria, and she is kicking her legs while sitting on the wall and then she walks to gather the toys. She can only get a couple as the other kids are faster, but to her, she was participating. It is success, but man, it hits you right in the gut how different your little one is in these moments. You never know when it is going to creep in just enough to leave you emotional and almost paralyzed. Aria needs water safety, and I fully believe being with her peers is best, not in the lower preschool levels with much younger kids, so that means here we are, facing the challenges head-on. Will we go for extra practice on our own? Of course. Will it continue to be hard? Yes. Does Aria need to work twice as hard to gain an inch, not a length? Every day. Does my heart feel exposed in moments like this? Excruciatingly so.

If you are wondering, there are other pools that do have classes that are geared towards what most know as special needs children. We don't currently have that option in our smaller town, which is why understanding the possibilities of an inclusive community is a passion of mine. Inclusive communities aren't simply about making everything accessible for all but also a mindset where we celebrate what we can learn from "all." It's about understanding what success looks like for each individual and celebrating together as a community. Right here, in those words, is where I heal and adjust my perspective. Aria wasn't looking at her peers and realizing that she wasn't floating on her tummy holding the wall and kicking. Aria was smiling at Mom as she kicked her legs, followed instructions, and splashed her favorite person. Tweak the perspective, and there was a lot more success than I originally let myself feel that day.

Often, as people, we shy away from the unknown or choose to be a silent bystander when we encounter something that may make us uncomfortable. Think about the amount of times you avoided saying hello to a person who displayed unique needs, or "special needs," as it is often referred to. It's okay! That is a natural response to uncertainty. This is where the power of Aria lies. She is a game changer and has this magnetic force about her that draws people in! She is showing our community the power of leaning in and considering what might be possible if we open a door. This is why we are choosing to share Aria's journey with the world. What lies ahead for Aria is anything but normal in many people's eyes, but here is a great quote by Maya Angelou we turned to for strength: "If you are always trying to be normal, you will never know how amazing you can be." Aria isn't alone in the need for a community to truly see the amazing individuals within and what they can accomplish.

If we consider the story from the pool, what could have helped? This is where we lean into the possibility of what an inclusive community could look like. What if, on that day, a mom told her child to say "Yay, Aria" when she found a toy underwater? What if the instructor came over and said, "That is a great adaptation of the kicking exercise" (even us parents need a little lift)? What if a mom told her child to "help" Aria find the last toy because she isn't as fast as them? This is what builds connection, understanding, empathy, and helps celebrate each person.

If you search for inclusion on your computer, you will come up with a variety of choices, definitions, and ideas. There are quotes galore and an ideal that feels warm and fuzzy. Inclusion is work. It is intentional work, and it is rooted not in a place but rather the culture. Who is responsible for culture? We are, the people, the community. Aria deserves a future where she is seen, accepted, and encouraged to reach her full potential, and although I understand I am a huge advocate for her, it's the community that holds the greatest power. Take, for example, our hockey community and the one junior hockey coach and general manager that invited Aria to attend practices a couple times a week. This small nudge opened up Aria's language skills, use of her communication device, and brought joy to a hockey bench of young players. Often, they would ask when she was coming; she could say the names of players before even "daddy," and even took to the ice when she turned 5 with the support of many. Aria started on a hockey sledge, but after watching her peers, she was on a skate trainer in no time. We definitely had to help the organization with how it might look for Aria to be in hockey, but no one ever doubted if she belonged there. You can see her infectious smile from the stands when she was on the ice, and this continues to this day.

Inclusion can be held in three words: community, sense of belonging, and identity. The opposite to this, and what inclusion is not, is location, compliance, and existing. When we compare these sets of words, we can really consider what inclusion means. For Aria and others, it's a place to grow, a place to belong, and a place to foster her identity. The community, whether it is the school, city, or sports, provides Aria with the ability to be an engaged member. I'm sure many of you have this goal for your child too. School is a location, but the school culture of inclusion is the community Aria is growing in. When students in Aria's class participate in a simple activity that says, "My favorite thing…" Instead of just the adult speaking for Aria, her peers answer the question. Simple! Meaningful! Empowering others to be the voice of inclusion is fostering the foundation of a strong community.

The hockey rink is the location, but our hockey association

and the Camrose Kodiaks (Junior A Hockey Team) are the ones who know Aria loves a fist bump or her favorite goal song or the ability to hug her favorite player. When she dropped the puck at the Stollery fundraising game the community understood why the goalie (her billet brother) took the face off. Collectively, our hockey family has encouraged the entire community to consider the slogan "hockey is for all" in a much different way. Aria is teaching others patience, sportsmanship, and perseverance each time she takes to the ice because, for her, it's twice as hard.

Identity is really knowing who Aria is and what she loves. Ask yourself a simple question: Are we asking kids to comply in different settings or embracing their identity? This is all about equity in my mind and understanding what a child needs to learn! If a student with ADHD struggles with remembering the steps at the end of the day, are we simply "telling" them what to do over and over again? Or do we find visual prompts to aid the process? If sports is part of Aria's identity, is her school community embracing this in helping her reach her goals? Currently she has double Physical Education class each day to help encourage social skills and gross motor development. Aria also loves animals, which was the driving force behind her companion dog through the organization Dogs with Wings.

Lastly, and the most important component of inclusion, is belonging. Above all, we want Aria to belong, feel welcome and cared for, and be in an environment where she can grow. Isn't that what all parents want for their children? Now, we know Aria doesn't "disrupt" the learning environment or community spaces, which can make it easier to embrace inclusion. But, for students who do struggle with behaviors, loud noises, or more complex needs, don't they deserve the same? Inclusion isn't about letting them in the room; it's about understanding how those around them can lean in with support and foster a culture of belonging. Showing people they do not need to navigate it alone and as a team we can overcome limitations. It's seeing the possible!

Being vulnerable, sharing my voice, and even putting my own words in writing is immensely difficult. Aria is my why. Each day, I am blessed to work with kids of all kinds. Diversity is truly a gift and to have the ability to authentically help others through my own stories is a privilege I do not want to waste. Each of my daughters, my husband, and our hockey billet kids have also learned through Aria's lens, and even though they might not know it now, they will be game changers in the years to come! They walk into spaces with a different lens and so can you. They see barriers to knock down versus limitations. Are you seeing the possible? I challenge you to consider who might not be accessing their community the same way we do for Aria. Many families are nervous, scared, or unsure of how to take a step to help bring their child into the community. Whatever the reason, we as communities need to lean into the idea that inclusion is possible, and it's not necessarily a location but rather a place we belong. Aria feels connection through simple gestures, and she knows an authentic lean-in when she sees it. Can you do the same for others in your community?

One strong advocate can push through many barriers, but imagine the power of many. Some days, advocating for all kids, especially my own daughter, can be draining. But I also know it's a path I was meant to walk. As Douglas Adams once said, "I may not have gone where I intended to go, but I think I have ended up where I needed to be." Where I have needed to be is sharing the notion that we don't always need to be alone in our advocacy, that others deserve to be part of this journey. Inclusion is not defined by a physical space but by culture and the sense of belonging it fosters. A person can feel profoundly alone in a room full of people if there is no true connection or recognition of their worth. Accessibility goes beyond ramps or entrances—it's about the willingness of others to notice, to step in, and to offer a hand when needed. The greatest power lies within us, in our ability to look beyond limitation and rather see the possible.

ABOUT ANDREA GUTMANN

Andrea Gutmann is an accomplished educator and dedicated mother of three daughters. As a school principal, she brings her passion for inclusion and community building to the forefront of her work, inspiring both students and staff alike. With a master's degree in education, Andrea has devoted her career to fostering supportive learning environments that empower all students, regardless of their backgrounds or abilities.

Her commitment extends beyond the classroom, as she advocates for her middle daughter, who has a rare genetic diagnosis. Through this personal journey, Andrea has become a powerful voice for awareness and advocacy, sharing her daughter's story to inspire others with her resilience and strength. She believes that every child deserves the opportunity to thrive and works tirelessly to create spaces where diversity is celebrated.

You can connect with Andrea for speaking engagements or more information at:

Email: ariasinclusivepossibilities@gmail.com
Twitter: @andreagutmann

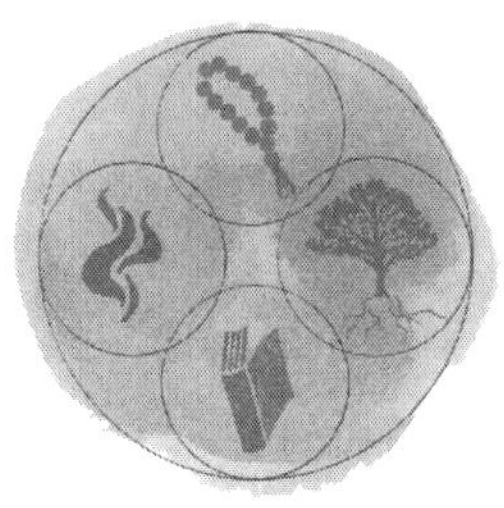

I AM A BRIDGE

Kelly Kinney

Abandoned. Adopted. Adored. Accosted. Addicted. Lost. Found. Rooted. Rising. Flying.

Come, take my hand, and at each bridge, from head to tail, I will lead you upon my Truths Trail.

My first language was astrology. And when we meet, it is usually the first conversation you have with me. I was born under a waxing 1/4 rising moon in Virgo, the Sign of the Priestess. In the month of May when the earth is in bloom and fairies play.

The elements had just crossed the celestial bridge, passing its burning torch of activation from abundant Earth Taurus to the mercurial butterflies of Gemini.

All the while, Scorpio was on the rise, over the horizon, imbuing my divinely human stardust with the mysteries of the dark.

The sun was sinking into the underworld, hovering its last sweet rays to shine upon the brow of a babe born with the gift to be a bridge between worlds.

With the light and dark, I was marked.

At the time of my birth, the planet Uranus struck its lightning bolt in the sky, branding me with its psychic and tornadic energy.

Out in a land where blue skies stretch far and wide and the sound of clicking heels rings in your ears when the wind blows by. Liberal, (Seriously, IKR!) KS just happened to be a passing by town to my biological parents, that now holds the key in the turning point of my Origin Story.

I don't think we are in KS anymore, Toto . . .

ABANDONED

This portion of my personal mythos I know . . . t's the first three years in human form that I have no real grasp for. Born to a couple who had lost their way and tried desperately to cling to life without drowning from their own pain.

I only have breadcrumbs from some about what the time looked like. Being abandoned many times only to be saved by Sophia's Grace and brought back to the safety of my paternal grandmother and auntie.

My grandmother, Iris, a feng shui master and astrologer for nearly five decades, was a powerful person to me while growing up; she seemed to embody truth. Not the candy-coated kind. But the raw, honest TRUTH. Though she was known in the family and community as "the crazy lady." She once feng shui'ed the homes of the Dallas Cowboys and was featured on Good Morning Dallas News; imagine that! No one even knew what it was then! She paved the way. I could see myself following this path.

Iris and Chiffon, too, were struggling to survive the tides of this human ride. My grandmother, on her own for the first time and fully sober for the first time in her adult life, caring for an infant. My auntie Chiffon in the throes of puberty. It was too much to bear, so Grandma rang her oldest daughter, Noelle Joy, a mother to three boys and the one to nurture each member of the family, all seven (including her own mother and father), into a state of safety and established being, along with her husband, Fred, who became my daddy. Their home and embrace became the sanctuary that would house many.

ADOPTED + ADORED

Noelle had already overcome so much in her life, raising her mother, father, brothers, and sister amidst the chaos of generational alcoholism.

Finding Fred at 17 and starting her own family, she birthed three sons.

She embraced me as her miracle daughter.

She says there was no question when the call came through. She would board a plane and gather her sweet miracle babe in the land of Texas and bring her home to the East Coast of NJ.

WE are DEFINITELY not in KS anymore, Toto . . .

But my childhood was far from perfect

I came in with my own language . . . No one could understand me until about the age of five when speech therapy started and lasted till the age of 12.

I can remember the way the sound would reverberate off my bones . . .

It was light language.

Soul song.

(I rediscovered it while in a shamanic rebirthing journey on my 36th birthday!)

ACCOSTED

It was the summer of my seventh year that the Cicada Brood X (the wing tattoos on my forearm signify the initiations this totem has taught me), which hibernates for 17 years, came through. My room peered into the woods behind my house. My safe place of rest, solitude, communion, and magic. I would stand within the trees, and the waves of sound would wash over and cradle me. Their tune, a tale of how we are all alive with the Great Mother inside.

That summer marked the end of an era. For when the season would change and the underworld comes to reign and we would gather for grace, my sweet body and soul were initiated through yet another gate of transformation as I was molested by a trusted extended family member.

Let's just say shit went awry.

I had to repeat the first grade.

I lied about EVERYTHING.

Or did I?

The switch in my body was flipped, and I was acutely aware of pleasure in ways my mind would take decades to understand

I could see the ways in which webs of fear and lies were threaded through the minds of adults everywhere!

When people would speak, I could see and feel their words reverberate through my being in the color of their purity and authenticity. And when it was lacking or riddled with trauma, it was shown to me in shades, smells, and visions I could not erase from my third eye.

I would shapeshift and energetically play with the light of their soul within the grid lines of source within.

Being a bridge composed of the elements of water and wind, I would blow truth back in.

With much of my goddess gifts activated at such a young age and being marked by the redhead flame (in the '80s may I remind you:).

It was a bit of a curse within a blessing for me to learn belonging within my own being.

So began my journey as an outcast, an abandoned, left behind, ludicrously marked redhead. So much cultural shame to navigate at a young, tender age.

My secret wound and marked wildness and known abandonment would shadow the days of innocence and play.

I often sought solace in the soil of the land that held me. The way the rays of the sun would beam upon my body would fill me back up with love, where the world slashed at me for being so loudly Me.

The evergreens that lined our driveway were my ever-steady

soldiers standing guard to protect me from all harm. I would crawl under their large boughs of arms that gracefully and heavily kissed the ground below. And begin to climb and slide myself through the inner forest of sticks, sap, needles, and bark. I would climb as high as I could and peer out from the perch to observe my home and its flow.

Not realizing then that my sweet body bled from all the scratches mixing with sap and mother matter, making me a eucharist for the great Mother in those moments of communion.

The summer came that marked the arrival of my moonblood, and the trees were cut to pave way for a smoother driveway.

I was officially a woman at 11.

This is when the visions intensified . . . Timelines shifting in and out of waking and dream time. Deciphering reality from what was behind my eyes proved to be a feat in and of itself.

With her pip, tough toes, in tow, most summers I spent with my grandmother, circling and vending at New Age Fairs, Holistic Health Fairs, and Metaphysical shops. Learning the tarot at nine, being Reiki attuned at ten, studying crystals and unseen energies. Her friends, cleansing my aura, teaching me about the magic of plants, ritual, and ceremony.

My grandmother only spoke of astrology, energy, sacred order.

An Aquarian way ahead of her time.

All of this led to the cultivation of my entrepreneurial spirit of creating sustainability for my existence by my own means provided to me.

I started a babysitting service and underground teen magazine and was working nearly every day but Sundays starting in 5th grade.

I tasted independence early, and it's still my most favorite flavor :)

When back home in NJ, the way I would continue to commune with spirit looked different. For Noelle did not learn from her mother the way I would come to.

She was weary from raising three boys, being a Cub scout mother and Sunday School teacher. When it came time for me, she allowed others to lead. She was fine as long as I was attending some kind of church each Sunday.

I continued to be a shapeshifter in my life. In between friend groups, I knew everyone, and they knew me. Some quivered, some snickered, some slammed me every way they could, trying to see if the redhead flames could be provoked. Some invited me in, only to cast me outside their circles, publicly, while playing with me secretly.

I spent many weekends sleeping over at different new friends' homes. Granting me the opportunity to go to their families place of worship. Raised Presbyterian, the chilliest sect in the line I know:) I became exposed to many, many teachings: Methodist, Baptist, Catholic, Jewish, Born Again, Jehovah's Witness, Hinduism, Buddhism. Before the age of 13, I had immersed myself in as many sources teachings as I could get myself to.

Reading Joseph Campbell's *The Power of Myth* at age 16 solidified my knowing that ALL IS ONE.

My school days were laced with initiations of rejections and suffering.

It was a confusing, isolating, igniting, and deep-diving time.

I grew up with a name different than was on my birth certificate as only legal guardianship was granted to Noelle and Fred. But my "real" name loomed like a shadow each first day of school when the teacher would call the roster and stop at me, reading and processing what they were supposed to do, which was ignore the legal name and call me by my chosen family name.

Sometimes, they would slip and say them together. Children would chuckle and make comments under their breath. Not knowing how to hold the moment of someone who had been unchosen, then chosen.

In my teenage years, it manifested as eating disorders that left lasting damage to my body. I did not feel like it was safe to speak my truth. Honestly, I did not think anyone would believe me.

When I received my license at age 17, signing for the first time my birth, given, legal name, the swooping of the second K AND the Y at the end seemed to lift a cloak, a veil from my essence. I had to speak it, on its own, and never did I hear my voice say my name. It reverberated a truth through my bones that had me walk a path into the unknown to find my roots and claim my story as my own.

I secretly applied to a private Catholic college, was granted financial aid, and went my freshman year to begin studying Mythology, World Religion, and Women's Studies.

I was taught by nuns who saw the sacred flame behind my blue eyes.

MM, some would say, then wink and walk away. I would not understand what they were referring to for another seven years and still uncovering more today.

I was too close to home though. My three brothers' protective presence weighed down my wild spirit from flying as freely as it desired to.

I craved to look into the eyes of the humans who made me. At least, the ones I thought made me. That's changed drastically along this journey of becoming.

I was careful as I did not want to cause alarm or harm my parents for seeking a truth they had saved me from.

So, I plotted with my auntie Chiffon who still lived in Dallas, TX. The last place where both biological parents were.

I transferred to the, University of North Texas, with a scholarship and financial aid. Purchased my one-way plane ticket. All on my own, informing my parents there was nothing to worry about as I was moving in with Chiffon and going to a great university!

It didn't go over so smoothly. But what could they say? They raised me with wings, and I was flying free, no matter what. Right into the life they pulled me from.

ADDICTED + LOST

There was always this shadow growing up that I would "end up just like them." The ones that "made me." Addicted and a drain to family and society.

So naturally, my trauma led me back to the beginning. To fulfill a whispered prophecy. Little did I know it was not the whisper that led me . . .

The trauma I carried found outlets, which we know is what happens when we don't have the proper channels to heal, and at that time, I did not have the knowledge, resources, or awareness level to begin unpacking my trauma.

There, I reunited with my grandmother and began exploring my roots.

Meeting my biological parents was both enlightening and painful. It mirrored parts of myself I

didn't want to see, but it also revealed my resilience.

It was then that I met Ben. The lines of fate wove a story that connected how we circled each other for decades, unknowingly, like in that movie *Serendipity* . . .

A story worthy of a chapter on its own, although tragic, more like the movie *Blow*.

Once found and love discovered, it was a sharp left in the direction of repeating generational trauma through addiction and a fulfillment of that whispered prophecy.

We found ourselves homeless and in the barren lands of west TX.

In a moment of desperation, I prayed for divine intervention—and it came in THE MOST surreal way.

That experience ignited a change . . .

I began to understand my power in a different way.

And so did Ben and those around me.

What I prayed for was insane in the moment it was happening. And it happened upon the breath that left my 22-year-old, devoted lips, quivering in trust to the Divine Spirit that lived within . . .

It pulled us out of that darkness, eventually bringing us back to the East Coast, where, with the help of my beloved family, we rebuilt our lives.

Although I felt FOUND, Ben's addictions would morph into a slow alcoholism that mirrored my biological parents' story.

My power was being siphoned in malicious ways that began to forge an exchange of generational pain.

Timelines shifting with stories repeating. My Virgo Moon, with my Scorpio third eye, could see the ties that did bind. Here is where I thought my namesake, Kelly Gaelic—meaning warrior woman, was to be claimed, and I would save him and thus heal all lines.

I took up the spiritual sword and shield and devoted my life for another 20 years to trying to save him but only saved myself in the end.

FOUND

Back to returning to the East Coast . . . Once safe and secure and snuggled into an apartment of our own with thriving promising jobs and no shadows chasing . . .

I became pregnant.

With my Virgo Moon and Venus in Cancer, I poured my energy into learning nutrition, yoga, chanting, breathing, and using all the tools my grandmother gave me to vibrate at my highest while gestating this force of creation within me.

My first born, Kaia, arrived on 11/11/04 and ignited a spark within the dark chambers of my heart, illuminating my womb, where the mother wound left another key to the unfolding of my story.

When a woman who has been abandoned and adopted by her mother gives birth and steps into that sacred role, it is a whole new healing in and of its own.

Postpartum riddled me.

It just happened to be the year Mary Jo Codey, wife to NJ Governor, began a campaign that unmasked the truth behind PPD and created avenues of aid for women everywhere and ignited a change in the face of maternity care.

That birth I knew could have been different. I was hungry to know how, and it ignited me along a path to discovering how I could heal EVEN deeper, for now I had this blue-eyed baby staring back at me.

I've always had the visions, the dreams that showed me what would be coming next, what to look out for, and when it would appear or materialize before my very eyes, but even I had trouble believing.

I started studying with my grandmother more.

Her death right after Kaia's first birthday would propel me further along into my fate.

I began to pray for a mentor.

Many women appeared whose gifts and talents wove into mine and brought a balm to the witch wound that plagued my heart at that time. Grandma sent every one of them.

I was easily the youngest in many a circle I was welcomed into. Most women my senior by 13 to 40 years! I was often told I was an "exception" made. When it was relayed , always through a sly smile and tilted head, a spark in the eye that said, "we see you," was silently conveyed.

And so, at the age of 24, I began my journey to self-discovery through modalities that lit me up!

That served to heal me first, my daughter next, and then all who would be open. Seven generations forward and seven back.

The holistic and mystical training I have received could fill a book on its own! As later discovered, high-functioning ADHD has been a superpower enabling me to have built the life of my dreams!

Through the study and practical life application of astrology, nutrition, massage, energy, herbs, crystals, anatomy, birth, breath and oracular magic, I opened Mother Earth Body + Energy Work when Kaia was only four years old.

Through this service work and while constantly being guided along my path with mentors at each turn who tended the divine feminine flame with care and love . . . My powers of touch and sight increased exponentially.

The original innocence of those days when I would play within the gridlines of people's energetic blueprints was activated, and the coals of truth burned deeper into the living layers of healing.

As naturally as can be while being held in the grace of a coven of women and serving the community through my given abilities, I was asked to attend my first birth a year after opening my first Holistic Healing studio.

After that, I was hooked. A birth junkie. There was no bullshit in the birth room.

No masks, no facades.

I dove in. Headfirst.

More training that could fill a book.

Mother Earth Body, Energy + BIRTH Work was born.

I had already experienced being pregnant three more times. Although they did not end in the birth of a baby . . . on the fifth time, my second born child began to swell my womb and inhabit my temple body space.

RECLAIMED

Her birth was the first home birth I ever attended. But certainly not the last.

Kora Irisana, born 1/11/12. Her birth was a journey of reclamation. One of listening FULLY to the angels' whispers, divine knowing, and trusting with unwavering faith in the ability of my body and my truth.

At this point I had attended nearly three dozen women in labor, all within the bonds of the trauma ensued in today's health care model. I would be damned if I would allow myself to be held down again and not follow my body's divine truth. Knowing it came with the ability to birth without interventions.

The key was turned, and I began to serve in birth in a way that led to me speaking in summits, rallying at hospitals for evidence-based birth, and being an integral part of changing some laws on birth care protocols for the women of NJ.

I was raising my children as holistically as I could amidst a world that pressed back, serving at births, being an activist, running two massage studios, and constantly failing at saving my husband from himself.

It took many, many years to divorce and find a way to safety. I am still recovering.

I learned through my marriage and my healing practice . . . no one can save anyone.

Only YOU can save yourself.

And so, I did, again, as I had so many times in the past.

2020

We all hold the chapter to the incineration that occurred. I could no longer touch people. I could no longer enter a hospital to attend births. I could no longer bypass my needs by serving and pouring myself into others.

I was asked, "What is your heart's greatest desire?" and I can only name what would serve another. I could not bring it back to ME.

I remember that moment. How I crumbled to the floor gasping for air, fingers flailing to feel under my shirt the beating of my heart . . . "Is it still there?" I irrationally thought.

It beat so loudly that upon that thought, my ears threatened to burst from its pressure. The resounding sound as if the Wizard himself was yelling into his megaphone, "YOU HAVE FORGOTTEN ME!"

I struggled to find my heart's greatest desire . . .

I followed the only thing I had full gnosis of . . . My body.

It led me to a 21-day dance challenge.

Which led me to discovering another group of wild women mentors who have initiated me into the ancient ways of wielding body and flame.

A fire keeper. Flame tender.

ALCHEMY

When you learn to move with fire, pure presence is beckoned. Shadows are seen. Embers ignite sleeping dreams. You can no longer hide from your own light.

I was giving a three-hour long shamanic bodywork session when sources voice rang though crystal clear . . . "You are complete here. It is time to expand and extend this light to reach more than these walls can hold."

I stared into my gong . . . COMPLETE HERE??????

I felt like I was losing my identity.

I had to close. Listen. This I knew.

Seventeen years of serving and honing my craft. From the mountains of Vermont to the island of Kauai and dozens of places in between, I understood this was a closing.

However, whispers of magic on the wind blew into my wings as my fairy endeavors were growing.

You see, in 2018, along the path of Sisterhood in Birth with a chosen family that saw my worth, I was granted into a Fairy Ring that ignited me into the service of sparkling!

Some of my most profound experiences, connections, and divine moments have come as a result of my fairy work in the world.

When I talk about my work as a "fairy," know it is a way of being. A way of living in magic, of holding space for the wonders that most people overlook. This part of my life is about creating a

life that feels enchanted, even when things seem difficult or uncertain and sparkling others with the same essence through our artful, masterful, and proprietary Fairy Hair technique and experience.

When I first started embracing this energy, I didn't fully

understand what it meant. It wasn't just about wearing wings or being whimsical. It was about embodying transformation and healing in ways that felt beyond the ordinary. It helped me to prove magic in the mundane, quickly and joyfully! I was no longer in service to one's pain but rather to their JOY! It was about stepping into my divine feminine power and helping others reconnect with their own. I became a bridge for people to see the light and the magic they carry within themselves.

I've learned that transformation doesn't always look the way we expect it to, but it's always beautiful. The role of a fairy is to show up in places where light is needed, to help people rediscover their joy, and to remind them that they are capable of creating their own magic. It's about making the impossible feel possible, igniting hope, and showing people that they can choose a different reality—one that ignites them FULLY.

When I dance with fire, when I guide others through sacred rituals, when I'm tapping fairy energy and proving that magic exists, I am providing an experience that ILLUMINATES and IGNITES one's hidden desires. And that spark within is seen when the mirror shows them their sparkling reflection of beauty!

Devotedly and diligently building the fairy business one strand of hair on one head at a time while still serving in birth and massage led me to discover even more about my health, wealth, worth, and power in this lifetime.

I closed both studios knowing that the expansion I was being asked to embark upon would lead me to a dream I had once seen. A shop and sanctuary that would house ALL of me and serve as a taproot to the sacred for the women in the community.

In 2021, I picked up fire and flew fully, right into the heart of my dreams!

To be SEEN FULLY and allow others to be IGNITED in their LIGHT and BEAUTY is what my path is now about.

Through every training and initiation I have been graced and gifted with, it was first to serve myself. I quickly discovered through the many faces of healing, as I did when studying world religion, that ALL IS ONE.

RISING

After searching for nearly three years . . . wishes were answered on Samhain, Halloween of 2023. Angels and ancestors orchestrated the procuring of my NEW space in NEW HOPE, PA!

When the address was sent through, 9 East Bridge St, my hands shook, my heart quickened . . . You see I have known for time before comprehension spelled it out for me, that I am indeed a BRIDGE.

Born on a cusp, all astro lines weaving the light + dark . . . My 3 leased past Studios . . . all located on a Bridge St, next to a River. I also have lived on a Bridge St, next to the river for the last 9 years. #9 is completion. And Magic of the highest as no matter what you multiply it by, 9 always returns to itself.

I parked on the other side of the bridge in Lambertville, NJ. The meter had exactly 44 mins left on it, the number of angels. I began to walk across the river water that sparkled a path before me, I can hear my Angels whispering along the winds of change, "Take root." they said. Looking down, ginkgo leaves, fairy bricks of gold lined the Bridges Path to the front door. Tears welled in my eyes as my womb pulsed with the knowing, that this was the one, my dreams were unfolding.

Filament fate lines wove well wishes for a future filled with MAGIC and SPARKLE!

As a holistic practitioner in the old, wise woman ways, flame-keeper, and fairy by trade, I'm honored to share my knowledge of my journey's secrets!

In the realm of sound vibration, herbal and floral remedies, flame, and sparkle!!!

My roots in New Hope run deep, and it's a dream to build this space to ignite and inspire you to live well, take great care, and SPARKLE ON!!!

New Hope is a homecoming!

I found herbs in this town when I was a young maiden of 17.

I have sat by the river as so many past versions of myself.

Creating The Wild Way ApotheFairy has been one of the greatest lessons in Believing BEYOND! In fact, BELIEVE BEYOND became a mantra to me while taking the year to create it as my angels deemed fit. Built by my blood, sweat, tears and the donations of those who believed in the beauty of my dreams.

Expectations smashed, gifts revealed, a new understanding of what it means to "show up" gleamed.

It doesn't make sense that someone of my stature, class, past would be a shop owner in one of the most beautiful and reputed towns of river magic there is.

I opened my doors on 10/11/24, as we know I tend to give birth on portal days.

On opening day I danced with flame and called my mother, daughter, sisters, and mentors forth and planted the sparked seed that The Wild Way-Apothefairy would be the taproot to house the remembrance of the magic we are all made from.

To serve the women of the community through every age and stage of their becoming. From Maiden to Mother and Crone.

A container to house all the myriad of ways in which I have served. To be the sanctuary where other women feel safe to open and heal themselves through the gifts inherited within.

The Wild Way beckons you to come and play as you once did when innocence reigned and your spirit was untamed.

To find the remedies which bring you into alignment with the Divine FAEminine flow. Where magic is all you know.

Miracles and magic are in every moment, and you hold the key to your own story. Turn the lock, set your soul free, speak your TRUTH, shine brightly.

In Faith, Love, Trust, + Pixie Dust,

Fairy Kelly

ABOUT KELLY KINNEY

Keeper of the Sacred Sparkle

Kelly Kinney, creatrix of The Wild Way ApotheFairy in enchanting New Hope, Pennsylvania, is a weaver of light and shadow, bridging the seen and unseen. With deep reverence for life's mysteries, Kelly guides transformation by blending ancient traditions with modern magic. Through her heart and hands, she shares wisdom gained from lifetimes devoted to activism, birth, herbalism, holistic body and energy work, sound healing, and ceremony. As a Fairy, she offers clients a tangible reminder of their inner sparkle.

She is pure magic—her powers are vast and transformative.

Kelly's life journey, marked by miracles, magic, resilience, and devotion to truth, has taken her across the globe, deepening her connection to the rhythms of the earth and cosmos. Weaving a web of women together to resurrect the red tent. Living along the Delaware River with her children, she spends her days dancing. You can sometimes find her spinning fire and silk while communing with fairies at the rivers edge

Kelly calls seekers, dreamers, and wild hearts to reclaim their beauty and power. Whether weaving intention into shimmering strands or igniting transformation through ceremony, she proves that magic lives in the mundane and that healing can be profound and playful.

To work with Fairy Kelly, visit:

Wildfirefairyhair.as.me

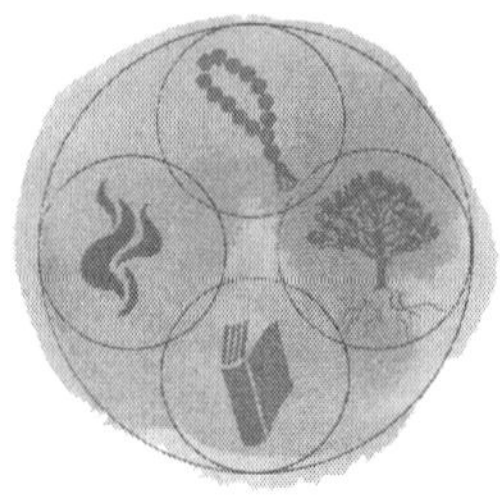

INHALE FOR LIFE, EXHALE FOR DEATH

Nora Rose Mogielski

One early November morning, my dad called us to his bed. My mother gathered us in their bedroom, which we converted many months ago. He knew he was dying and wanted us to be with him. The room was quiet. He lay there in a hospital bed, surrounded by the things that had always made him feel at home. His favorite hat on the dresser, his newspaper and reading glasses on the side table, and my mother sometimes wedging herself between the rail and him, except not this day. I held his hand, the warmth of it fading into mine when he asked, "What will the nuns say?" His voice was faint but still recognizable, still the voice I had known all my life.

He had worked at St. Joseph Hospital for years, devoted to the people there and to the mission of care and compassion. Now, as the cancer slowly took him, he seemed to be seeking some reassurance, some last comfort. I squeezed his hand, trying to steady my own emotions. "They'll say you're going to heaven," I quivered to him. He had always believed in the goodness of God, in the quiet grace of the nuns and their prayers.

He turned his head and looked at me, his eyes sharp for a moment, as if trying to make sense of the tears on my face, and asked, "Then why are you crying?" His voice was a whisper now, as though he didn't want to disturb the stillness that had settled around us. I looked at him, my heart breaking, but I couldn't stop the tears, "Because I'll miss you." I said, my voice breaking. And it was true; I would miss him with every part of my 18-year-old self. But I also knew that in this moment, he was at peace. His suffering was over. And yet, I couldn't bear the thought of him leaving his young children. He looked away and up as if he understood. We made him as comfortable as we could, adjusting his pillows, anything that might ease his way. There was nothing more to do except to be there, to hold him, to remind him that he wasn't alone. I was thankful that we were all together—him, me, my mother and sister, the people who loved him most.

As time passed, the sound was unlike anything I had ever heard before, like a coffee percolator softly bubbling, a low, rhythmic gurgle rising and falling in my father's chest. It was the sound of a body letting go, of life slowly slipping away. The death rattle. But he was no longer in pain. Not in the way he had been, fighting cancer for the past six months.

The last breath left his body quietly, and just like that, my father was gone. But at that moment, I didn't feel alone. There was a strange peace in the air, something I could not name but could feel in the marrow of my bones. As we stood there in the room, holding on to him, his body began to shift. There was a faint, brown liquid at the corner of his mouth, the last sign of a body that had fought so hard.

And then, just as I looked down at his face, his eyes closed, his features calm as if in sleep, the light in the room changed. From the window, a beam of white light poured in, brilliant and pure, casting a glow across his still body. It was a flash of brightness, almost too perfect to be real. And in that moment, I knew, I could feel it; his soul was leaving him, following the ray of light out the window. It was as though the light itself was calling him home to heaven.

I watched as the hairs on my father's arms stood up, as if his body, too, could feel the presence of something greater than us in the room. The air grew heavy with something sacred, and though I couldn't explain it, I knew we weren't alone. Something divine was here, in that space with us, guiding him on his way, his body at peace, at last. My dad, in his wisdom, had left us with this beautiful gift. Being with someone as they pass is an honor I will always cherish.

My mother, in her strength and wisdom, knew exactly what needed to be done in those final moments and beyond. She called the priest at our church to come to the house to bless my father. He gave a personal reflection about his home experience at mass that day. My mother handled everything with such ease and grace, even through her pain and tears. It was an extraordinary experience that taught me a powerful lesson. Life must be lived fully every single day. When you're lying on your deathbed, it's too late to make changes, too late to chase dreams. Time runs out. So, go after what you want, make mistakes, learn, and start over if you have to. We are here to enjoy life, to live it to the fullest, to discover our gifts, and to share them with the world.

For most of my life, I lived fully, pursuing my dreams and embracing life's experiences. That changed many years later when my mom passed away. It devastated me in a way I never anticipated. In her final years, I moved her into my home to better care for her, taking her to doctor appointments and monitoring her health closely. After a surgery, she was transferred to a rehab facility, where her condition began to decline. She was agitated and didn't want to talk about her feelings or what she was seeing. The next day, around 2 a.m., she asked the nurse for orange juice because she felt dizzy. I knew she wasn't ready to leave this world, but by 7 a.m. on that cold January morning, she took her last breath.

I hugged her tightly and cried, thanking her for being the best mom I could ever want. At that moment, I felt heartbroken and overwhelmed by guilt as her caretaker, wondering if I had done enough, if I had been there for her in all the right ways. It's a grief that I carry with me still and a love that will never fade.

As I waited for phone calls, I reflected on the past two weeks with a whirlwind of emotions. We celebrated my daughter's college graduation, and my mom was overjoyed to be there with us. It felt almost like divine intervention that my daughter graduated early, a blessing that I hadn't fully grasped until now. I did my best to make the holidays memorable for her, cherishing our time together. I never thought those would be her last moments with us. But reality has a way of slapping you in the face, and now, I find myself feeling incredibly alone, no longer a daughter with parents to lean on. I don't know how to cope with that. The finality of it. That this is it. There will be no more late-night phone calls, no more advice, no more of her voice telling me everything would be okay.

In an instant, everything changed, and there were so many decisions to make, with no time to think. Where do you want to take her body? What about the obituary, the funeral, the wake, the burial? Pallbearers, the casket, the clothing, every detail rushed through my mind. My mother and I discussed her wishes for these arrangements, but now she was gone, and the weight of it all had fallen on my shoulders. I never imagined it would feel this heavy. I don't know where to turn or who to ask for help. Every decision, every detail feels urgent, like it must be done immediately. But how can I possibly be the one to handle all of this when, inside, all I want to do is collapse and scream? It's as if the world is spinning around me, and I'm powerless, trying to breathe through the overwhelm.

Grief consumed me, and depression tightened its grip as I faced a bitter, below-zero winter. Like the weather outside, my heart felt frozen, scattered into shards of ice. I was paralyzed, unable to move, my body heavy and numb. To calm myself, I meditated in bed, trying to find peace in the chaos. During this time, I discovered Jack Canfield's events, which became a lifeline, guiding me through the darkness. It wasn't easy. It was work. But I knew I had to help myself, had to claw my way out of the state I was in.

So, I set new goals, made new friends, and pushed myself to the extreme by jumping out of an airplane at 15,000 feet. Yes, skydiving. I threw myself back into life in a way I

never imagined possible, and in that freefall, I felt a strange connection to my mom, as if she were right there with me, soaring through the sky. It was a leap into the unknown, both literal and emotional, but it was exactly what I needed to begin healing.

My parents' deaths were so different, yet each one taught me profound lessons about life. Even now, I still talk about the love and kindness they gave me, keeping their memories alive by celebrating them with my family. We eat at their favorite restaurants, prepare their favorite meals, plant trees in their honor, and listen to the music they love. When I see butterflies flutter around me or dragonflies stick to my shirt, I feel a gentle reminder that they are nearby, watching over me. I write about these experiences to honor their legacy and soothe my soul.

Today, my life is thriving again. I have three grandchildren and one on the way. They give me a new existence. New life and death are the parallel between the act of breathing and the cycle of life. These new little lives, the moment of coming into being, are the inhale, the oxygen, the receiving, the energy, and the presence of breathing. With each inhale, we are nourished, filled with life and love, and connected to the world around us. While death is the exhale, the release of breath, the last breath, a return to something greater than ourselves. We inhale when we are born into the world, and we exhale passing from it.

Together, "believe beyond" unites the cycles of life and death with the belief that there is something beyond our limited understanding, a purpose that connects everything, even in moments of loss and grief. Accept the invitation to live and face death with faith that there is something deeper. My parents' death experiences have shown me this.

I share this with you because grief and healing are deeply personal journeys, and we all have our own way of honoring and remembering our loved ones. It's possible to live both grief and joy simultaneously when we express ourselves and know their love is always with us.

Whether you've lost a home, a job, or someone dear to you, grief creates an emotional wound that requires healing. Everyone will face it at some point in their lives. There's no escaping it.

In those times, normalcy may shift in ways you can't control, and it may take longer to return than you expect. Be patient with yourself and others. Show empathy. So, take a deep breath in; life begins again; start with small steps, create a simple plan, and take it one day at a time. I suggest following the three C's: Choose, Connect, Communicate.

Choose what's best for you at this moment. Maybe it's signing up for a class or taking a trip. Connect with those who will listen and who will offer support without judgment. Communicate what you need, and most importantly, talk about your grief. Share your story. Let those who care about you hear it and allow them to love you through it.

Surround yourself with people who lift you up, who encourage you to share memories, and who understand the process. Before long, you'll begin to see positive changes. New experiences and new people will enter your life, and slowly, you will begin to lift yourself up, finding your way back to a new version of you.

Be kind to yourself. You'll find your strength again, and you will move forward.

ABOUT NORA ROSE MOGIELSKI

Nora Rose Mogielski is a coach, speaker, and the author recipient of the Parent-Teacher Choice Award. She offers author visits for her children's books *Gabriel's Journey, A Journal, a Recipe, and a Family in America*, and *Bentley's Week*. She has co-authored several books, including the #1 best-selling *Goodness Abounds, 365 True Stories of Loving Kindness and Faces of Grief.* Nora offers meditation and vision board goal-setting workshops to schools and group events. She was the business owner of Roots & Wings Child Care Center Inc. for 22 years and still does consulting. Nora is a teacher who inspires leadership skills, fosters confidence, and encourages the understanding that learning is a lifelong journey. Through her guidance, students not only develop the tools to lead but also embrace the idea that growth and learning extend far beyond the classroom, continuing throughout their lives. She is a Jack Canfield Success Principles Certified Trainer. She holds a Bachelor of Arts in Education, a Master of Arts in Curriculum and Instruction, and a Master of Arts in Health Communication from Marquette University. When Nora is not writing, she enjoys reading books, water sports, kayaking, playing with her dog, and traveling the world with her family.

Instagram: @nmauthor
Email: norarosebooks@gmail.com

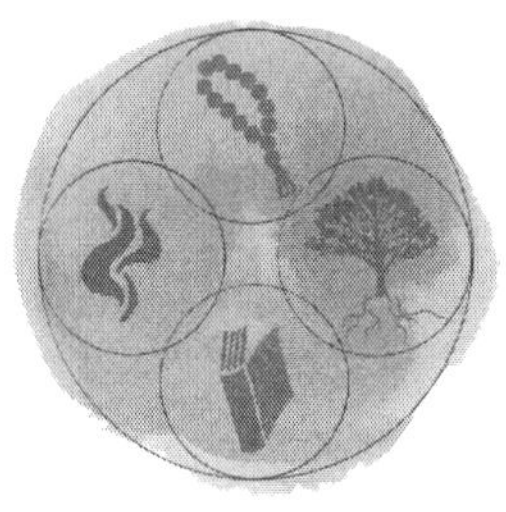

BECOMING A STAR

Tiffany Star

"Too Tall Tiff," she said with a smirk as she walked away. The words pierced through my body, and I felt the blood rush to my face. I just stood there in embarrassment. I couldn't wait to get to basketball practice; it was the only place I didn't stand out and where being tall was okay. Inside, I safely tucked and locked away all of the emotions and beliefs of not being good enough, pretty enough, or worthy enough, thinking I was somehow protecting myself from being hurt again. I put on a smile and pretended I didn't care, letting three simple words from my young middle school years define me.

I allowed these thoughts and feelings to join forces over the years with all of those voices . . .

Get back in line. Don't do it that way. Do it this way. That's not right.

You're too happy, too loud, too sensitive.

You laugh too much, smile too much, talk too much.

You need to learn this way, look this way, dress this way, talk this way, connect to God this way.

You can't do that.

You dream too big; you'll never have that, be that, or do that.

. . . filling up and locking my heart with distortion . . . thinking if I stay small and don't shine my light too brightly, people will like me.

***

It wasn't until I became a mom that my life completely changed. I discovered there was something greater than me now. I saw how deep and miraculous love could be as I stared at this beautiful being that somehow came out of me.

In my eyes, she was perfect, a clean slate. Then, the fear washed over me of not keeping her safe. I desperately offered overprotection, watching every move like she was made out of porcelain . . . breastfeeding, reading, cloth diapers, organic . . . trying to be perfect to mask all of the worry and panic. Trying to quiet the voices of that Tall Girl inside me.

Then, one cold, silent night, as I laid there with my 8-year-old daughter sweetly sleeping snuggled up beside me, my heart filled with sadness. Despite no ringing sounds in the air, she was still at peace. I tried not to let the promised phone call bother me, admiring how strong my daughter was. *Why was I so weak?* I needed to stop being so selfish. I should stop making excuses and feeling sorry for myself. I needed to stop feeling like I wasn't good enough, pretty enough, or loved enough. The divorce was already over with more painful emotions and all my secrets safely tucked away within the confines of the now massive wall built around Tall Girl's heart.

I laid there questioning myself. *Is love a weakness? Is forgiveness a weakness?* I let go out of love and to offer happiness, but things were exactly the same as before the divorce. I'll always love and forgive. *Is that right or wrong?* I kept pressing myself for the answer. I gazed down at my daughter; my heart sank as I thought about her future. An electric rush came over me; a fire ignited inside; energy filled my entire being with love, power, and determination. I knew what I needed to do.

Mixed tears of emotions flowed down my cheeks. It was so clear and simple. *If this was my daughter, without question, I would tell her to leave.* Feeling stronger already the words echoed through my head, *The divorce was over,* remembering I was blessed with one gift . . . our daughter. We were free to leave.

We both were able to walk away, both still being Stars. Thank you, sweet ex, for the three gifts for our new journey: our daughter, your name, and growing into strong "Stars." I am forever grateful. I could stand a little taller and one day say "I did it" to my daughter as we drove away.

***

I was empowered, strong, and determined to give my daughter the best life possible. Our new life was exciting, joyfully combining work, homeschooling, and fun. It lasted a while until worry about being able to say "no" for fear of letting people down or making them upset slowly became an issue. Not following my heart, along with aiming for perfection and pleasing others, made me spiral downward and make decisions that would affect not only me but my daughter as well. The guilt, shame, and disappointment consumed me. I began to break down until I could barely do anything physically, let alone help others, which I so desperately wanted to do.

My whole body was crying out to me. I didn't want to know what was wrong with me. I already knew there wasn't one single part of my body that wasn't in pain; the list was endless. At age 44, I looked like I was 88, and I felt even older, my spine curled forward, bedbound, and unable to stand. I laugh at the thoughts of that young Tall Girl and how beautiful she really was. I would love to have just one feature of hers to be mine in this monster I was now hiding inside of, with hair and skin falling, large sores breaking . . . now hearing the voices . . .

You're doing it wrong. Disgusting. What's that? What's wrong with you?

. . . appearance was the last thing on my mind, now trying to block out all of the rumors, the looks and still be strong. Why aren't they able to see it is the little things that they do that help transcend me . . . the love, encouraging words, and kind little jesters, each more powerful than any lost time spent on judgment, stares of disgust, and gossip? I was a Falling Star trying my best to belong. I knew of the Law of Attraction and the thought of the mirror of what I was projecting saddened and worried me even more, a vicious cycle and reminder of what I was capable of.

Despite all of this, the one person who could see my beauty was my daughter when it should have been me. She always wanted to take pictures to remember each moment, whether it be the most joyous or less than joyous "one we will laugh at later" moments. She could see through it all and tell me my eyes were so pretty; they're so blue and bright. She found the good in me. *Why couldn't I?* She was a true role model, and I knew that we were going to be alright.

Then, one night, my life was changed forever. My 16-year-old daughter came into my room and woke me up. She told me that when she was lying in bed, she lost her breath, and it felt like everything inside of her left her body like she was an empty eggshell. "I saw the most beautiful place. I felt happy and wanted to stay," she said as she continued to describe it to me. "I knew I couldn't because I needed to come back to help you get better." My stomach dropped, my heart melted, and I felt my entire body heat up with mixed emotions of fear, worry, and love. Thankfully, she was okay, and I am forever grateful.

Enormous amounts of guilty emotions filled me. My daughter came back for me. *Why was I so blessed with such an amazing daughter with so much love for me?* I didn't know why, but I knew that I had a lot of thank yous to send to the powers above me. There is something much greater than me. It was time to stop wallowing in my pain.

I started to get stronger and made the decision that no matter what, I was determined to get my daughter to a six-day home-school convention and graduation that I had been planning for her for months. It was her chance to meet new friends and go to prom. I knew it was going to be life-changing for her. Using a board, I slid out of my bed into a wheelchair and to the hotel.

"Declined." Panic shot through me like a lightning bolt; temporarily held incident charges put me over the credit limit needed to make this whole experience happen. I could not let my daughter down again. I somehow figured it out and was able to make the graduation trip a reality.

On the last day, my throat was on fire, and I had liquids coming out of both ends of my body. Thankfully, with that power from up above, we made it home safely. We were greeted by my mom, but I was too sick and dizzy to fully engage as I tried to quickly let the patiently waiting liquids release from my body. Little did I know this would be THE turning point in my life; third time is the "charm."

May 30, 2024. My body was already numb from my own pain. Somehow, I knew this was coming. I couldn't feel anything. I didn't want to feel anything. I didn't want to talk about it. I couldn't. It didn't seem real . . .

"Mom died," uttered my dad as he opened my door. I couldn't speak, and I couldn't connect.

As the days went by, I couldn't push it away any longer; the reality kept creeping in and becoming stronger. The sounds down the hall that I thought were my mom were just the sounds of the house. I felt lost, scared, and broken if my mind tried to think of her. She was my partner in pain, and we were going through much of the same. The only way we could communicate at times was through texts. Little did I know that the day I came home was the last day I would see her. She was so happy I made it home safely. She was proud of me and told me I did a great job raising my daughter. I went back and forth, wanting to look at the texts, to hold on to her final words; it felt comforting, but yet at the same time, too painful to enter that domain . . .

"I kept thinking of your words 'God wrapping me in warm light' when it was rough last night."

"I think of you all of the time and pray it is going ok. Are you sleeping in a bed or wheelchair?"

"Remember God's warm, loving light is surrounding you."

"Thanks, if you were here, I would cry with you."

"I hope you are doing a little bit better today. Love you, and you are on my mind and in my prayers." "I can't come in and see you. It's been a rough day."

"Love you so much."

. . . I know that my mom is watching over me, shining down from the stars above. I will hold on tight to her love for me.

I realize how important it is to enjoy and cherish every present moment in life. I now see what I have right in front of me: a beautiful daughter inside and out with immense love for me. I am inspired to be the best mom I can be. I now see that it isn't all of the "things" that make it so; it is me bringing the most joy, love, and happiness to every present moment that I possibly can . . . breathing in the fresh air, feeling the gentle breeze, listening to the melody of the birds, smelling the flowers, soaking up the rays of sunshine, gazing up at the stars and talking about our dreams, all that we can have, be, and do together.

I am faced with a decision right now. I have three choices . . .

I can give up, I can stay the same, or I can start living and try.

My time is right now; no more excuses. This is not the end of my story; it is just the beginning of what I can achieve.

I Can Do It. I am going to Dream Big, laugh too much, smile too much, play, and be happy. Be me. I

am doing it right. I am beautiful. I am free. I love you, Tall Girl; you are precious to me.

I am going to stand up tall and let my light shine brightly. From now on, I will follow my heart, taking comfort in knowing

I can call for guidance and support from above, listening closely to that soft, gentle voice of love. With a song in my heart and that voice in my head, I choose a life filled with smiles and laughter . . . love, joy, and fun.

I have *StarPower,* my own unique gifts to share with the world. I believe all things are possible, for I am a Rising Star.

What is your *StarPower*?

Join me on this epic mission to conquer the biggest challenge of my life. I am going to "heal, stand up, and walk" again. We can shine our uniquely beautiful lights brightly together.

We are awesome. We are victorious. We are Stars.

. . . to be continued

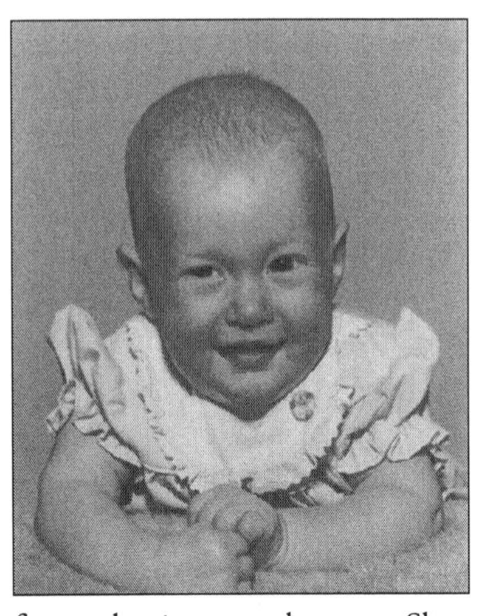

ABOUT TIFFANY STAR

Tiffany has a BS in Exercise and Sports Science (specializing in management) from Iowa State University. She has a background in massage therapy, sales, counseling, hotel conferences, nursing home CNA, lifeguarding, and pet care.

Her varied experiences in life have given her direction and guidance in her aspirations of helping others through future business endeavors. She wants to continue to write adult, juvenile, and children's stories and open up a healing company.

Tiffany is going to "Dream Big" and awaken that child inside who dreamed of becoming an author and one day having her writing come to life on screen through motion picture films.

Tiffany resides in Florida. She loves the beach, nature, animals, reading, and exploring diverse cultures.

If you would like to join Tiffany on her mission to "heal, stand up, and walk" and want to shine your light with her, she can be contacted at: whatisyourstarpower@gmail.com.

Feel free to send encouraging messages, share with her your own journey and dreams, tell her what your *StarPower* is, or just say hello!

StarPower—our own unique gifts and talents, using them to do what we love, bringing us joy, happiness, and the authentic fulfillment of our dreams.

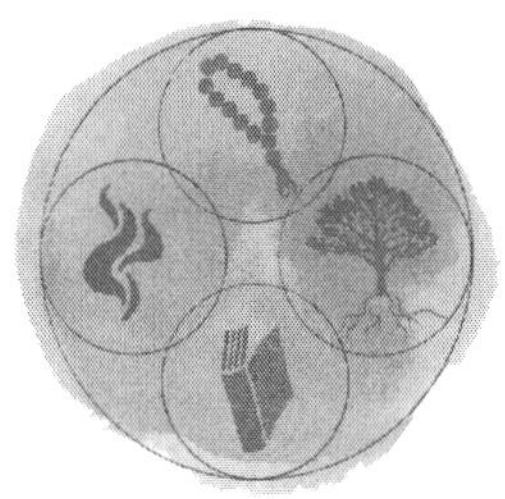

THE ROAD FROM SUPERFLUOUS TO SUPER BRAVE

Anne Tyler

Have you ever wondered, "How the hell did I get here?"

I've found myself in that same place too many times to count.

I looked around at my life, my house, my body. All the evidence I'd been avoiding, ignoring, blocking…had become blatant, loud, door-knocking style, screaming signals of what wasn't right, what wasn't aligned. Everywhere I looked was a reminder. I know *why* I avoided and ignored these things. I did it for safety, I did it out of fear, and I did it because of overwhelm.

I thought about all the things I'd been tolerating. They were starting to scream at me once again. They'd done this before, but I had felt I couldn't handle them, so I kept on avoiding and ignoring. I didn't trust that I'd be able to take care of the things. I told myself I didn't have enough strength, I didn't have enough money, I didn't have the time, and that I didn't have the competence.

I'd gone numb. Going numb is nothing new. It's a skill I've learned that's probably helped me in many situations. But going into this state for too long and too often begins to have its consequences.

If you would have known me 25 years ago, you would have found someone excited about the future and eager to take on the world. A much braver, bolder me.

Around that time, I was at the beginning of my career in radio as an on-air personality and was living in my first apartment with my daughter. The apartment wasn't perfect. It was the cheapest apartment I could find at the time within a neighborhood I knew was relatively safe. The main building didn't have locked access. One window in my apartment was off its alignment and didn't fully shut (which is a real bummer in Minnesota winters). When I told my landlord about the window, he matter-of-factly advised that I could turn on the oven and leave the door open. YIKES.

On the door to my apartment, skinny yellow stickers with the faint words, "Police Line Do Not Cross" decorated the door frame. The landlord had also informed me there was a pimp living in one of the first-floor apartments.

I was broke, but I was proud of that apartment and hopeful about the future. Luckily, it was shortly after that I was offered a position for my own radio show in another nearby town and moved into a much better apartment. In this apartment, there were two bedrooms and TWO bathrooms! One for each of us! It felt like such a big deal. I had my own laundry room, there was a big balcony, and it was a nice space in a great location. I felt even more proud.

I wanted to be a good example for my daughter and show her that you can go after things you want, even if—or especially if—they are outside the norm. Pursuing something like radio was not anything like what anyone else I knew was doing.

Unfortunately, it was also around this time that the relationship I had been in for a year slowly started showing signs of trouble. Looking back and knowing what I know now, the red flags were there. I was in love, and I wasn't prepared for what would ultimately unfold. I'd like to say that was the end of that part of my story, but it wasn't.

My intuition was starting to first whisper to me, then tap me on the shoulder, then it started screaming at me. But by then, I didn't know how to get out. I had knots in my stomach, I was often holding my breath, and my body was in a constant state of fight or flight.

There were moments where I'd gone numb and checked out instantly, and others where it was a slow process. It makes me think of the story of the frogs and a hot pot. The story goes like this: if you were to put frogs into a scalding hot pot, they'd jump out instantly. But if you were to put the frogs in a pot of cold water and slowly increase the heat, they would become acclimated to the heat, bit by bit. All the while not knowing they were being cooked to their death, until they were too weak to find a way out. So, they perish in silence.

This is much like "grooming" in an unhealthy relationship with someone who means harm. You don't know it's happening until it's too late. When you're in a relationship with someone who has unhealthy intentions and is using various tactics like love-bombing, gaslighting, bread-crumbing, and unpredictable silent treatment—you start to feel isolated, defeated, and can eventually feel a slow, eroding loss of self.

Recently, I was watching the movie *Elf* and there's a scene where Buddy says, "I don't belong here. I don't belong anywhere." Santa says, "Christmas spirit is about believing, not seeing." I thought about all of the times I had felt like this, like I didn't belong.

Your belief in yourself is everything. This dictates how you act, what you don't act on, how you carry yourself, what you'll go after, and what you won't. My belief in myself had waned.

To come back into consciousness, you have to be willing to really look at who you really are. How you really want your life to be. And how you want your life to be might be completely different from anyone around you.

Avoiding and numbing can seem like the only way to cope, and maybe it is in the moment. But when it goes on long-term, it's just plain exhausting. Not allowing, or feeling safe to allow, your authentic self to come through takes a lot of energy. And when you're exhausted, it becomes a vicious cycle. It makes everything harder because all of your energy is spent in coping and handling hard things. It leaves less energy to take care of yourself in basic ways. Your sleep patterns are off, you feel too exhausted to exercise, and everything hurts.

In my own state of numbness, I watched as all of these things happened. I had checked out, and it affected everything. I was someone who normally loved exercise. I loved my hip-hop workouts, Pilates, and good ol' Tae Bo (it's still a damn good workout, y'all). I was someone who ate healthy, but had a good balance and indulged appropriately for my body. My favorite indulgence was always brownie dough. Everything in moderation.

I've always been a night owl, but over time, I felt like I never really slept well. I had let that slip, too. Being in a numb state, I felt like a zombie. So exhausted yet I would have a hard time getting to sleep with my mind running nonstop. I was so exhausted that I couldn't think straight. This would also make me so restless and have OCD about things before going to bed. This meant checking the locks and checking that the stove and oven were off 20 times. My mind had become cluttered.

One night, while in the kitchen doing the usual OCD routine, I thought about how I had recently noticed that the floor tiles had matching pieces throughout the flooring. I'd never noticed this in 13 years of living in my house. This may seem like a mundane thing, but it also meant something else to me.

It was a real "huh" moment for me. I thought about how funny it was that I was spending time over this revelation that there were duplicate tiles. I noticed how the different speckles in the design were consistent in some of the tiles.

Then, the word "superfluous" popped in my head. I don't remember what made me think of that word. I thought, "Is it suPER-floo-uhs, or is it super-FLOO-uhs?" I couldn't remember, because who uses that word? Well, I had been lately.

According to CollinsDictionary.com, it's defined as "unnecessary or is no longer needed." Synonyms include: "excess, surplus, and redundant." Yep, I looked it up in that moment. Then I thought, "How numb can I be if I'm spending a moment contemplating the specific technicalities of tiles and the word, 'superfluous'??"

To me, this was a sign that I could let go of all of the chatter that had haunted me from the past. It was time to shed it. I didn't need it. I had finally been *able* to start doing so. It had slowly been happening, but in this moment, I *felt* it. I'd been feeling braver and bolder again, especially in the past year. I had decided I was done putting my life on hold. I had recently *really* thought about how getting older is just getting older. I didn't want to just get older. I wanted to come back to my true self and go back to my original dreams.

I couldn't tell you the moment I decided I was over it. Over the numbness. There were so many little moments this decision bubbled up inside of me. It was definitely a matter of two steps forward, one step back. Sometimes it actually felt like two steps forward, three steps back. How does that math work out?

That's how it felt. I knew I wanted to feel like my braver and bolder self again.

I can tell you that I started honoring what I wanted, my unique view of the world, and what I truly valued. It wasn't perfect. It was more of a hit-and-miss kind of path, and looking back, I don't know if it could have been any other way.

It was the small things. Like watching a movie I wanted. Stopping at a little store that came to mind. Going on a deep dive rabbit hole researching something that was interesting to me.

The biggest decisions came with trips that filled my soul. I followed my gut and took some risks in making these happen. Some of these included trips where I could learn from major mentors of mine firsthand, like Lisa Nichols on a Mexico personal retreat and in California with Jack Canfield to become certified as a Success Principles coach. There were many others like this.

In the space between where you've been and where you'd like to be, there's a gap in identity. It's a space where you have to decide how you're going to bridge the gap. Who you think you are versus who you want to become. It's about being in integrity with the one you want to be. How can you show up as the new, or uncovered, braver self?

If I could go back to that girl 25 years ago, here's what I'd want to tell her to keep her braver, bolder self. Maybe you need to hear this, too:

Get out asap.
Get out of the relationship.
Get out of the friendship.
Get out of the job.

It doesn't get better, it gets worse. Trust your intuition. It doesn't feel right because it isn't right.

Save some of the money when you have extra. Your goal is to have at least six months of savings. It's true what they say. The money will give you a different sense of freedom and purpose. It will give you the ability to walk away faster from things that are toxic. Call it your "get-the-hell-out-when-I-want money." Remember, freedom is your biggest motivator. You don't like rules, and you don't like feeling tied down. There's a reason. Honor it.

Forget what everyone around you expects you to do. Forget what everyone around you thinks you should do. You know what you should do. You know what you need to do to move in the direction of what you want. Do it. One baby brave step at a time. Your boldness is still there.

Don't shrink to make others feel comfortable. Their insecurities and lack of consciousness are not yours to take on. It isn't your burden to carry.

This one is big. Read it again. Come back to this often.

Keep dreaming. Keep dreaming those big, crazy dreams. It's the crazy ones who actually make change around here. Block out time for this. This is a priority. This is what's gotten you the crazy things no one thought was possible.

If others aren't rising to their higher selves around you, don't lower your vibe to make them feel comfortable. It's sucking the life out of you.

Let yourself have fun. Remember, it's one of your biggest values. Don't let others around you believe that having fun and getting things done are mutually exclusive. It's a lame belief and just plain untrue. You get shit done when you're having fun. Let the right people come along for the ride. Let the rest sit there and watch you shine. The right ones will come around.

It's not your burden to wait around for them to get this truth.

Keep your deep sense of curiosity and sense of playfulness. You honor and love others who possess this quality. This is a wonderful trait that makes you, you. It makes your soul happy and helps you follow your genius natural intuition.

Don't take in the lies that are all around us in this world. They originate from unoriginal ideas from people who don't take time to question the "norm."

Remember this question—since when are you a rule follower? Some traditional "rules" just don't even make sense. Some are downright ridiculous. Am I right??

Be your weird self. It's your gift. It allows others to show their weird, too. It sure makes life way more fun.

FEAR. You're human, you're gonna feel it. You live in a society that's intent on cultivating and creating fear. It's in our advertising. It's in our movies and TV shows. It's in our social media. It's perpetuated in our families and in our homes. A lot of it is swirling in our heads, weighing on our hearts.

I've heard people say that FEAR is False Evidence Appearing Real. I recently heard another version even more empowering: Face Everything And Rise (Zig Ziglar).

Now go get 'em, and go create the thing! You already know what to do.

ABOUT ANNE TYLER

Anne Tyler is a certified *Canfield Success Principles* trainer, speaker, and coach based in Minneapolis, MN. She's on a mission to help women entrepreneurs shake off their doubts, step into their brave selves, and claim the bold, authentic lives they deserve—one "baby brave" step at a time. With a mission to help women feel seen, heard, and deeply understood, she works to guide them in uncovering the authentic, fulfilling lives they are meant to lead.

Anne loves nothing more than being in the company of strong, heart-centered women who share her vision of lifting others up. Whether leading workshops, speaking about personal transformation, or sharing heartfelt conversation over brunch, she is always drawn to meaningful moments that celebrate connection and courage.

Anne believes that when women support each other, incredible things happen. Her work as a trainer and coach is a testament to her commitment to creating safe spaces where women can rediscover their inner strength and begin building the life of their dreams. Her message is clear: courage doesn't have to be loud to be life-changing.

She is a proud mom and grandma to the loves of her life—two amazing daughters and two wonderful grandkids who keep her very busy.

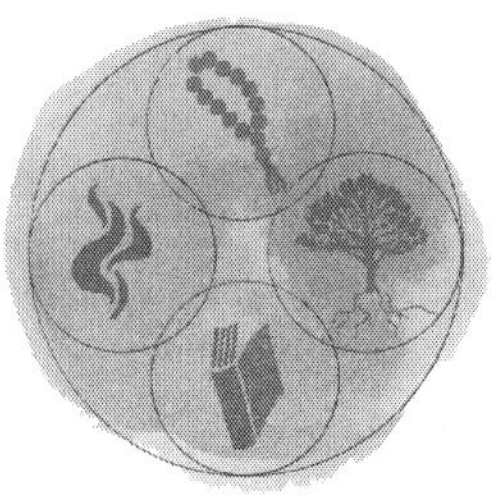

THE LEMONADE LIFE

Eleni Yiambilis

Isn't there just something about waking up in a hotel that hits a little differently? Perhaps it is the fluffy pillows or the fact that you do not need to make the bed. Whatever it may be, there is an undeniable ease and pace that feels lighter than the daily morning routines at home. A hotel reboot This was exactly the vibe I was seeking after the weekend my daughter and I had experienced.

However, the ease of the morning on July 22, 2024 was quickly halted. The day ahead would forever change our lives.

The sun was shining in through the window as I laid in the bed. Deep heart-centered breaths activated my energy for the day. I smiled as the light warmed my face and I began reflecting on my daily gratitude. I remember wanting to add a sprinkle more ambiance to the moment.

"Ah, music! Yes! Music, that is exactly what this moment needs!" I thought to myself. I laid there and scanned the possibilities for meditation tunes in my mind. I grabbed my phone from the nightstand and squeezed the side buttons to turn it on. The black screen illuminated with the iconic white apple. Something screamed urgent in the pit of my stomach as my eyes digested my notifications . . . 47 missed calls and 88 new messages. I opened the text messages first.

"Eleni, where are you? Are you ok?" -from a neighbor

"Eleni, it's Jeremy from the fire department. Call me as soon as you get this."-a firefighter friend of mine

"Eleni, your house is on fire." -from another neighbor

A numbing shock ran through me as I hit the dial back for my landlord, who had called close to thirty times.

"Where are you?" She asks.

"Zoe and I needed a little peace; we stayed at a hotel. What is going on? There was a fire? How bad was the fire? What room?" I asked with a nervous curiosity

"Oh, honey, not just a room. It is gone. It is all gone. The house completely burned down last night. How far are you? Let me come get you." She replied

I assured her I was fine to drive, and I would be there in twenty minutes. The numbness turned into a buzz throughout my entire being as I hung up and looked my 8-year-old daughter in her eyes. I paused and took a deep breath, not knowing exactly what to say or how to say what had happened. I chose to be direct and I said to her

Zoe, our house burned down last night."

Her eyes seemed to get as wide as frisbees, and I could feel the shock emanating from her body. Her first thoughts were panicked inquiries about her pets. "Where are my cats; where is Zeke? Mommy, Anthony was in my room."

I asked her to say a prayer with me. I remember it being a quick praise to the Lord "Thank you God for keeping all of our pets safe"

I told her we would see everything when we got to the house and we would keep praying for the pets, but we needed to get moving with no delay.

Riding down to the lobby in the elevator, I knew in my soul we had an important decision to make. A choice that held within it the power to impact the direction of where this situation would lead us, for perception is power.

I looked at Zoe, and I said, "We have a path to choose. We either decide right now, in this moment, that this is God working a miracle for us, and we feed this with every fiber of our being, or we choose to believe that this is the worst thing that has ever happened to us. Either way, it is ours to decide."

Before the words came out of my mouth, my choice had already been made. This fire was somehow life happening for us. I was fully conscious and intentional with the words I was choosing and the meaning I was giving this situation. I anchored my belief that this was a gateway for miracles. Miracles so big that I could not even fathom their impact yet. The blessings that would come into our experience as a result would be God's ultimate validations. I knew a redirection was happening that would catapult us into accelerated momentum. We both agreed in that moment that this was, in fact, the Universe conspiring on our behalf. From that moment moving forward, "life is happening for us" became our mantra on repeat.

I really didn't know what to expect upon arriving at the scene. As we turned the corner onto Newell Road, I felt a gasp in my chest as the air was pulled from my lungs. There is nothing that can prepare you for the devastation of seeing your home completely demolished by fire. Piles of black ash and rubble still smoking, firetrucks lined up and down the street, people standing all around. I parked my car in the driveway. The shocking reality of the severity of the situation brought me to my knees instantly. I did the only thing that felt right in that moment. I faced the house, and I put my hands in prayer. I invited my daughter to join me. "Zoe, pray with me."

"God, thank you. I know and trust that this is part of your perfect plan. That you are opening doors of miracles and blessings for me and Zoe. We are going to get to experience the love of our brothers and sisters in a way we have never experienced it before.

I know God, that you are going to work through our community to help us feel the love and support to carry through this. I know you are blessing us in this moment right now, and I call forth your good to be shown to me." I sat on the ground, rocked my daughter in my arms, tears running down our faces, and with all honesty, I tell you, I felt ZERO fear.

We stood up, and our dog came running to us; our cat Angel came from the neighbor's yard. The miracles were already beginning.

There was a slew of questions to be answered by investigators and living arrangements to be made quickly. People wept and held me in embrace. It was an enormous amount to take in conceptually

In the haze of what was happening, I found myself contemplating, "Do I share this on social media?" I knew one thing. I definitely did NOT want people to think of me as suffering or devastated. Being a teacher of the Universal Laws and a transformation coach, I have come to think of thoughts as investments that yield a return. We make these investments, not only for ourselves, but for other people as we view and judge their circumstances. I knew that by sharing my story, I would be opening myself up to be the focus of other people's thoughts.

The more I reflected upon this, the more passion pulsed throughout my veins.

"YES! I absolutely need to share this!"

I wanted people to be with me in this seemingly tragic event. I wanted them to see me choosing miracles. Choosing to see this as a springboard and God working in my life. It felt like an opportunity to me, an opportunity to show up and serve. Who could I inspire by sharing my perspective about the situation? How could this help someone else navigating life? Perhaps it could nudge them to give a different meaning to whatever they were going through.

Only a few hours after arriving at the house, I went live on

Facebook, standing on the burnt pile of soot. I opened my heart, and I praised, and I proclaimed that I was choosing to see this as a miracle that I didn't quite understand yet, and I was asking for their help. The best way to help me and my daughter in that moment was to believe with us. Believe that there were hidden miracles that would emerge from the ash. I asked everyone to expect the best for us. To continue to celebrate life together, no matter what the outside circumstances look like.

As the next few days unfolded, an overwhelming amount of blessings were bestowed upon me and my daughter. The community quickly rallied, raising funds and gathering all of our immediate needs. Two of my dearest friends came forward to help, one with a camper for us to stay in during transition, the other with a trailer for any salvageable items to be stored safely. All of our bunnies that lived outside were able to be rehoused. I rescued the surviving fish in three aquariums from the collapsed den and found them ownership. Spudnick the turtle was found on the back deck . . . ALIVE! He was released in a nearby pond. Three of the four cats had been found. My inbox had two new opportunities present themselves for speaking, a happy surprise unrelated to the fire. A wink from God. Messages of support were pouring in. People reached out expressing gratitude for my perspective and validating my decision to share our experience in real time as it unfolded.

Within a few days, a new home became available for immediate occupancy from the most generous family. Three weeks after the fire on my daughter's birthday, Anthony, the one missing cat, was located.

In the flow of miracles, I decided to focus my passion energy on creating. I discovered incredible joy in making custom hats. Out of that birthed a new business and partnership, Three Little Birds. One magic moment to the next, Zoe and I had the rare opportunity to not only meet country music superstar Lainey

Wilson but also gift her one of my custom hats and our best-selling children's book *I Am That! I Am!*

For me though, one of the biggest and most thrilling blessings has been the opportunity to go on a variety of different platforms to share my story in a bigger way. I know that my story can serve and relate to a variety of audiences. I can confidently say sharing my story is making a positive impact on listeners worldwide.

This is exactly what I knew in the moment I consciously chose the meaning of the fire. I knew this would create the space for people to reflect on how they are perceiving their own lives and circumstances.

This is my invitation for you, the reader. Take a moment and evaluate the meaning you are giving to situations not only in your life but the life of your fellows. Are you expecting the best for yourself? Are you expecting the best for others? If your neighbor tells you they have been laid off, what are your first thoughts? Do you expect hardship for the family? Or do you immediately see this as some sort of divine redirection that will bless them? Just because something has been devastating in the past for someone else does not mean that it has to be devastating for you. You can choose miracles. You can choose blessings by choosing the right thoughts. It is simple. Is it really a lemon…Sour to the taste? Or is it the ingredient for some refreshing, thirst-quenching lemonade? This, my friends, is living the lemonade life, and for me, it is the only way I live!

ABOUT ELENI YIAMBILIS (elenee yam bil is)

Eleni is the founder of Eleni.life. She is a mother, an international experiential speaker, transformation expert, 2x international best-selling author, quantum healer, and one of the creative geniuses behind Three Little Birds Customs. She is also the innovator and driving force behind The Empower Mentor Movement, a program that introduces positive mindset skills in elementary schools. Eleni is known amongst her community as the miracle manifester, which is not only validated by her own life but the metamorphosis her clients and audiences experience all over the world.

Eleni attributes the blessings in her life to the perspectives and thoughts she chooses.

"Somewhere along the way, so many people have forgotten that WE decide the meaning of situations in our lives. Perspective is a SUPERPOWER, and all we need to do to activate it is choose what aligns with our desires."

-Eleni

Visit Eleni.life to connect with Eleni, register for her upcoming classes, book her as a speaker for your next event, access her podcast library, or purchase her literary works:

I Am That! I Am! and *Women Who Illuminate*
Follow her on Instagram @threelittlebirdscustomaccents to check out some of her designer creations.

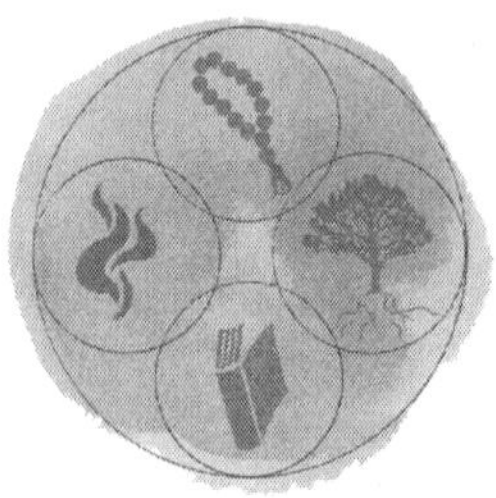

RISE WITH RESILIENCE: IGNITE YOUR LEADERSHIP IMPACT

Shanea Clancy

I want to take you back to a moment when everything felt uncertain. The weight of the world seemed too heavy on your shoulders, and you couldn't see how your dreams could ever come to life. You might have questioned if you were truly capable of leading, making an impact, or even surviving the challenges life placed before you.

I've been there. I've felt doubt, discouragement, and the fear that comes from standing at the edge of something bigger than I could have ever imagined. But here's the thing I want you to know: You were born for such a time as this. **You were born for this.**

You were born to lead, to rise above, and to develop the kind of mindset that transforms not only your life but the lives of those around you. The truth is, everything you need to make an impact, to be a resilient leader, to become the person you're meant to be, or ascend to your full potential and destiny—**is already within you.**

It's just waiting for you to tap into it. Dust it off. Unwrap it. Take it off the metaphorical shelf you have placed it on.

Ascending to Greatness: Master Your Mindset

Mindset is the foundation of everything. The thoughts you believe, the stories you tell yourself, and the way you see the world—**they shape your reality.** If you want to be a resilient leader, you must start with the most powerful tool you have in your toolbox: your mind.

I remember a time when I was stuck, paralyzed by fear. There was fear of failure, fear of judgment, fear of not being enough, and fear of success. I thought that leadership was reserved for those who were naturally confident, perfectly poised, or somehow more capable than I was. I grew up thinking leaders were born or passed the subliminal family torch of earlier successors. The truth is mindset mastery doesn't require perfection—it requires **awareness, intention, and the ability to adapt.**

The first time I went ice climbing, I faced an icy, imposing overhang that seemed nearly impossible to conquer. With each strike of my pickaxe, I had to push past fear and doubt. The numbness pierced my fingers and toes, accompanying exhausted biceps and forearms from clawing my way up the first 1,000 feet. Knowing that every move required precision, strength, and mental focus, I scaled, falling multiple times in an attempt to scale the icy overhang. I fell. Tried again. Fell again. Fell at least twenty times more, each time merely dangling from my harness and crampons. Feelings of defeat attempted to creep in each time. Anaerobic at this point, the cold wind howled away at my almost frost-bitten face. My muscles quivered. I couldn't afford to think about it. Instead, I thought back to the many hours learning how to tie knots, carrying a 200-pound pack uphill both ways, the hundreds of bleachers I ran, and the rigorous training I invested in up to this very moment. It was all in preparation for a time such as this.

Every swing of my axe, every step upward, demanded grit and fortitude. It wasn't just physical. This was a mental battle of internal dialogue to defeat my limiting beliefs. Each time I smashed my crampon into the ice to stabilize, I mentally smashed the internal negative dialogue. This was about mindset mastery. I knew I was strong. I knew I was prepared. I knew I would conquer the overhang before me and continue smashing away at the ice above, ascending to the summit. As I moved higher, the sense of accomplishment grew, knowing that each moment of doubt was met with another strike, another step. Reaching the summit wasn't just about conquering the cliff. It was about conquering myself, one pickaxe at a time.

The lesson I learned: You can change your life by changing the way you think. You can reinvent yourself and shape your future. Every leader, every resilient individual, has faced moments of doubt. But those who succeed aren't the ones who never experience fear—they are the ones who make the conscious choice to move forward **despite** it.

Mastering your mindset isn't about ignoring fear or doubt; it's about acknowledging it, embracing it, and harnessing it for encouragement by deciding that it will not control your actions, reactions, or destiny. When you can shift your focus from the doubt in your mind to the conviction in your heart, authentic transformation begins. This is the foundation of mindset mastery.

The Resilient Root: Leadership Refined in Fortitude of Adversity

Resilience is the root of effective leadership, especially for those who see leadership as a responsibility to others. Life has a way of throwing unexpected challenges our way, and the true test of a leader's character and heart isn't in avoiding setbacks. It's in how they navigate through them with humility, grace, and opportunity. The best leaders are the ones who not only persevere but encourage and empower others to rise alongside them.

I remember a moment early on in my career when everything I believed in seemed to unravel. The career path I had poured my heart into came to a screeching halt. The weight of failure was heavy. I questioned my abilities, my choices, my worth, and even my purpose. I felt like a failure who may never recover. It was in that low moment that I realized my next step wasn't just about me. It was about others, my family, my community, my peers, and someday, the family and children I hoped to have. It was about the example I wanted to set. It was about shattering generational barriers and limiting beliefs. I scraped myself together, making the conscious choice to arise. I felt and believed with my very core and every fiber of my being that there had to be more to life, that I hadn't yet fully tapped into my purpose and potential amidst this complex world.

Resilience in leadership is not about bouncing back alone. It's about being there for those you lead and guiding them through their own challenges. It's about offering a steady hand, acknowledging that setbacks are part of the journey, and just as important, if not more, than the bounce back. Resilience isn't just about bouncing back; it's about having the courage to get up again and again—to swing that mental pickaxe time after time. It's about encouraging others to see the opportunities for growth. Every time we rise after a fall, we show those we lead that they, too, can rise, pivoting with grace and agility while learning along the way. In the process, we become the kind of leaders who build others up, teaching resilience not through words, but through action.

Every setback is an opportunity for you to develop your strength, your character, and your resolve. Every time you get back up, you become more of the leader you are called and destined to be.

The Power of Posture: Leading Beyond the Frontlines with Purpose and Service

True leadership doesn't come from titles, power, or positions. We can be stripped of these at any given moment. Titles and positions are not meant to define us. It's how we lead with servanthood and intention that matters, and if it comes from the heart. When you lead from within and tap into your authentic self, you unintentionally create a ripple effect that inspires others to do the same.

A powerful lesson I learned along my own journey is that leadership is about **service**—not just being the one at the front but being the one who empowers others to rise alongside you, oftentimes, leading from behind. Leadership is about showing up. Not because you have all the answers, but because you're willing to walk with others, share the wins and losses, and get in the trenches.

This kind of leadership doesn't just change the trajectory of your life. It transforms the lives of those around you. The most resilient leaders are the ones who don't just push themselves to grow. They encourage others to grow too, empowering them to reach their full potential.

I've witnessed this within countless individuals I've had the pleasure of coaching and training over the years. Whether it's a client finding their confidence, a peer finding their voice, or someone in the audience feeling the courage to pursue their dreams, their life trajectory changes course. **When we show up as our true, authentic selves, we inspire others beyond their limiting beliefs to do the same.**

The impact you can have when you lead from the heart is immeasurable. Every small act of kindness, every word of encouragement, every moment where you choose courage over comfort, are the small yet significant acts that will leave a lasting mark on the world.

Dancing with Doubt: Turning Fear into Fuel

There's a common thread that runs through every person who has ever risen to greatness: the battle with self-doubt. You know the voice I'm talking about—the one that says, "You're not enough," "Who are you to lead?" or "What makes you think you can make a difference?"

But here's what I've come to understand: **self-doubt is a sign that you're pushing your limits.** It means you're stepping outside of your comfort zone, and that's where growth happens. The truth is, everyone who has ever achieved anything of significance has had moments of doubt, opportunity for growth, moments they've wanted to give up. The difference is, they didn't let those moments define them.

When I first began stepping into leadership roles, I doubted myself constantly. I feared I wasn't qualified, that I wasn't ready. But each time I chose to show up anyway, something magical happened. I didn't need to have all the answers. I just needed to be willing to **learn, to listen, and to act with courage.**

Self-doubt doesn't have to stop you. It's a signal to dig deeper, to challenge your fears, and to keep moving forward. When you face that voice of doubt and decide to act anyway, you create a new narrative—one where you are capable, strong, and worthy of the leadership role you're stepping into.

Courage in Motion: Bridging the Gap Between Vision and Reality

Vision is powerful. But without action, vision remains a dream. The gap between where you are now and where you want to be is filled with steps you have yet to take. So often, we get caught in the planning phase, paralyzed by the "what-ifs" and the fear of making the wrong move. But the most resilient leaders don't wait for perfect conditions. They act, learn, and adjust as they go.

The first step is always the hardest. It requires faith in yourself, in your purpose, and in the belief that every small action will eventually lead to something greater. Trust me. I've been there, staring out into the uncertainty ahead and wondering if I was making the correct decision. Each time I pushed through the fear and acted; I was one step closer to becoming the leader I needed to be.

Here's the truth: **Action fuels momentum.** The more you move, the more clarity you'll find. You may not always know exactly how things will unfold, but by taking that first step, you put yourself in motion. That is where the magic begins to unfold.

Rise, Lead, Thrive: Your Leadership Legacy Starts Now

You were made for more than just surviving. You were made to lead, inspire, and most importantly, thrive. Though the path may not always be easy, the mindset you cultivate today will shape your ability to be courageous and resilient tomorrow.

So, take a deep breath. Embrace the uncertainty. And know that every step you take—no matter how small—is a step toward becoming the resilient, impactful leader **you were always meant to be!**

ABOUT SHANEA CLANCY

Dr. Shanea Clancy is a #1 best-selling author and global speaker whose messages have inspired audiences at Fortune 500 companies like UPS, top universities such as the University of Pittsburgh and Carnegie Mellon, and 50+ high schools and colleges. Clancy has coached, advised, been endorsed by, and shared the stage with numerous top achievers including Demi-Leigh Tebow, Anne Beiler, Jeff Hoffman, Jack Canfield, and Jamie Kern Lima. She has been featured on FOX, Times Radio UK, PBS, CBS, NBC, and more, inspiring live audiences of over 65k+.

Clancy holds an RN diploma, BSN, Forensic Nursing and Doctoral degrees from Duquesne University, and an Executive MBA in Healthcare from the University of Pittsburgh. She's an Advanced Practice Certified Addiction Registered Nurse and Fellow in the International Academy of Addictions Nursing, with a deep commitment to mental health, restorative justice, and prison reform.

As a highly sought after expert in leadership, mindset mastery, addiction, mental health, and conflict resolution, Clancy is dedicated to empowering others to shatter limiting beliefs, ignite their purpose-filled passion, and maximize their full potential. Through Clancy Consulting Services, her books, coaching, consultations, and live events, she empowers individuals to create transformative futures filled with love, light, and leadership.

To learn more about how you can connect and work with Shanea, please visit her website at www.ShaneaClancy.com, where you can find her books, services, inspirations, and free gifts."

Connect with Shanea on social media @ShaneaClancy.

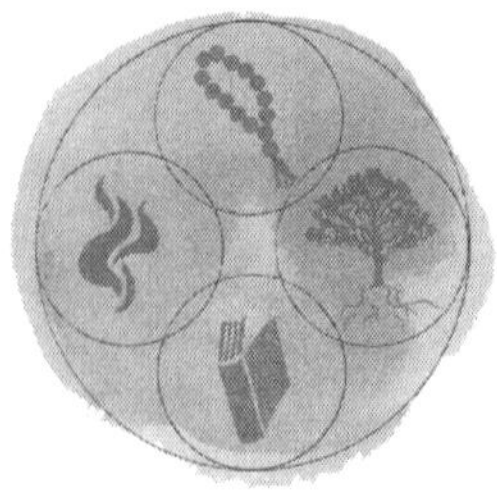

THE COURAGE TO BREAK PROMISES

Sarah Magill

I walked down the airport corridor wearing almost all the clothes I had packed. After backpacking for five months, mostly near warm tropical beaches, my body had completely forgotten it was raised in the Pacific Northwest. It was early March in Seattle, and I was effing freezing and completely at odds with myself.

On one hand, it felt like the right thing to come back home to connect with my family and best friend. I had mastered the art of vagabonding, making complete peace with the uncertainty of where my next meal was coming from or where I'd sleep that night. I assured myself I was just going to go back home temporarily. I'd reconnect with my loved ones and wait tables till I earned enough money to travel again. Not long since I'm the queen of travel hacking.

I came back from my trip with newfound confidence. When you land alone in a foreign city, can't read the signs, have no phone, and still manage to find your hostel, you figure you can do pretty much anything...especially waltz up to a gorgeous man knowing how much better his life would be if he had your phone number.

I saw him at Staples, the guy I dated in ninth grade. I

remembered him as the scrawny stoner who gave me pot for the first time, but now he was quite possibly the most beautiful man I'd seen in all my life.

"Hi, Leo. Do you remember me?" I knew he would, but I wanted to hear him say it.

After long walks, deep conversations under the stars, and lovemaking that transported me to another dimension, the rest, as they say, was history. We spent every minute of our free time together.

I had dreamed of having my own family, more like obsessed about it, ever since I could remember. I resented being a child of divorce, of being told my family was "broken." I swore I would do it "right". I would have a family, be a hot soccer mom, and drive a white suburban.

And here I had someone gorgeous, who had professed his love and devotion to me and seemed to want everything I wanted. Would I ever come across someone who would want this… with me?

"I definitely want to be more financially established and pay off my student loans before starting a family. Plus, you know I want to travel more and cement my career as a writer."

"We can do all of that together, mi amor! The time to have kids will never be perfect. We love each other and want to spend the rest of our lives together. You can do your travel planning magic to take us wherever you want, and I'll find work wherever we go. We can have adventures and still have a family. We can do anything together."

All this love-bombing made it really difficult to recognize some concerning behavior. Leo became incredibly angry when I had plans that didn't involve him or when I wanted to touch base with a male friend from high school. When we were at a bar with my friend, I sensed his quiet demeanor shift to brooding. When I asked him what was wrong, he spat, "Why do you have to check out every guy in here?!"

Despite all that, I was surprised he wanted to spend his life with me. He was gorgeous. In my entire life, I never had a chance with the guys in whom I was actually interested. Sure, he had a temper, but he was devoted and wanted all the things I wanted. I always heard that marriage was work. Maybe this is what they meant. I made a mental list of all the things that made him angry and tried to exist within those boundaries.

The next few weeks were consumed with the planning I'd always dreamed of. I quit birth control, and Leo got his passport. I used my points to fly us to Barcelona for $11 round trip and looked for work away jobs to cover our accommodations.

Walking into a pharmacy in Madrid and asking for a pregnancy test was exactly the type of scenario I imagined in my dream life abroad. We celebrated by looking over Madrid from the balcony in our hostel.

Traveling with someone so scared, angry, and insecure provided the opposite experience of the carefree adventures I had earlier that year on my own. Leo didn't handle changes well or when there wasn't a clear plan. We spent hours every day arguing. I thought, how can he possibly be mad so often? We're in *Spain*. We don't have to work, we're eating amazing food, and we're having a baby. Isn't that everything he could want?

After five conflict-ridden weeks in Spain, it was time to come home. We spent the night in the airport to save money. Even after I managed to fall asleep with all the noise, the cold from the floor snuck deep inside my body and woke me up repeatedly. I moved across the room to see if I could get settled on the chairs.

"How could you leave me over there?!" Leo demanded. I couldn't tell how long I'd managed to sleep this time.

"But baby, I was cold and couldn't fall asleep."

"Did you ever think how I'd feel waking up and not knowing where you were?" And so began another fight in one of the most beautiful cities in Europe. As the diatribe continued, I realized the severity and weight of my choices leading up to this point.

He was absolutely livid that his pregnant fiancée moved across the room to get more comfortable.

I considered losing him at the airport and getting a later flight. We were officially making a scene, breath and fury infused in every word, curses and insults flying. You would have thought I went home with the waiter by the sound of the tirade.

But what about the baby? I'd spent my entire childhood swearing I'd be better than my parents. I swore I wouldn't have a "broken" family.

This was a skill I would continue to develop in the coming months, withdrawing into myself when an unexpected conflict arose with no escape. I would use it when I left the laundry in the washer too long, wasn't in the mood for sex, or walked in front of the TV with wet hair (he was sure water would somehow get on the TV and ruin it).

In June 2015, my labor started. I was insistent on laboring at home with an experienced midwife, and if you've seen *The Business of Being Born*, you'll understand why. I picked someone I knew, someone who came highly recommended, someone who had over 30 years of experience.

After 55 hours of grueling, non-medicated labor and four hours of active pushing, my lips and eyes had swollen shut. I was so out of breath I could hardly manage to ask, "Are you sure it's supposed to take this long? Should we just go to the hospital to check?"

The midwife told us, "I know it's hard, but we have to do what's best for the baby, not what will give you the most relief."

Finally, my mother had enough and insisted we go to the hospital. Just before they rolled me into the OR, the entire medical staff stopped for a prayer. "Really?" I thought. Do we really have time for this? My mother bent over, whispered in my ear, and said, "Please, honey. Please accept the Lord into your heart and soul . . . just in case."

It was the nurse who told me the baby didn't make it. Leo

held my hand and looked at me, totally broken, tears welling in his eyes. His despair made him look so pure. This baby was the only reason I hadn't left him at the airport in Spain. I could leave this hospital a single woman. I could start over.

But his son just *died*! I could never be so heartless.

We went home together, moved across the state, started new jobs, and did our best to keep it together when coworkers asked us if we had kids.

The fights continued.

"Why is there butter on the half and half?!" Add to the list, "no butter or oil on any surface."

But he's grieving, I told myself. We all grieve in our own ways.

I almost left that one time he flipped me on the bed and straddled me with his hands around my neck.

I almost left the time he beat the dog.

I almost left that one time he screamed at me for stepping on his phone when he left it on the floor, and I couldn't see past my pregnant belly.

Every time a screaming fight threatened our future, when I would share that this can't be healthy, he'd say something like, "What would our son think, up in heaven? He'd be heartbroken." I couldn't bear the thought.

We didn't have family in our new town, but we managed to make some friends. At our last gathering, before our rainbow baby came, he invited me to the porch and smiled at me with the giddiness of a little boy about to play a prank. He said, "Mi amor, I want you to announce the baby's name to your friends."

"I thought that was still up in the air."

"I've thought about it, and you should be able to give the baby the name you love. Go in there and tell your friends we'll name our daughter Odessa Camille."

As far as I was concerned, this wiped the slate clean. I was ecstatic announcing to our friends the strong, beautiful name we would give our daughter. We'd been through so much together, and it felt like we had really turned a corner.

This time, I labored in the hospital, and it was a fairy tale birth. Leo was an incredible labor partner, reminding me of everything we learned in birth class, whispering to me in Spanish as if we were the only people in the room. This time, I pushed for just 25 minutes.

She was finally here. A shining success for arriving alive, for arriving vaginally after my previous C-section, for weighing in at the 90th percentile, for all her rolls and long black hair. She was perfect.

When all the nurses left, Leo stated he wanted to name her Quinn. "What about what you said at the party? I feel so connected to her as Odessa." The volume of the room changed instantly. I couldn't walk away with the epidural still in effect. I couldn't call a friend or, much less, the nurses. I was doing it again, drawing inward as he yelled until I caved. I couldn't bear the thought of the first sound to fall on our daughter's ears to be the sound of her parents fighting. I should just be happy that she was alive and healthy, and I wanted to rest so badly.

It was March 31st. Another fight started whenI cleaned with bleach instead of Clorox wipes. I tried to squeeze past him as he blocked the hallway. With my back turned, he shoved me to the floor. Immediately, I looked up and thought, "Did she see that?"

That's when I knew.

I was willing to deal with a lot in the name of family, but I was NOT willing to raise my daughter in a household where the mother was shoved to the floor.

Another episode of Sarah sobbing in a parking lot.

I called my best friend of 20 years. I was ashamed of what I had let my life become. I knew I was meant for greatness, but I was 25 years old and just waiting to die, waiting for all this to be over. I knew what was happening at home wasn't right, but I never talked about it.

"Sarah, why do you stay if you hate him so much?"

"I've already bought my wedding dress and put a deposit down on our venue. We have a daughter. I have to marry him."

She reminded me I did not have to marry him, that people break up all the time and for much smaller reasons than all the things I just mentioned.

"I can't raise my daughter in a homeless shelter. And I can't leave the dog there with him. I don't have anywhere to go."

"Sarah!" she said exasperated, "Why would you even think that was an option!? I will come get you! AND the dog! We'll figure it out!"

I truly had not considered that as an option. I would rather live in constant fear, managing the emotions of an unstable man, than ask my best friend of 20 years for a really big favor!

"Let's do it." With those three words, my life instantly became a box office drama, complete with the heartbeat in my ears and an epic soundtrack.

It was Monday. He left for work, and I watched him drive down the street. I made a cup of coffee as if this was not the day my entire world would shatter. The day I was running away, across the state, with a baby and a dog I never wanted. The day I say goodbye to my dream of having my family under one roof.

It killed me not to pack ahead of time, especially with all the baby gear. In every box office thriller where the woman runs away, she makes the mistake of doing it immediately after the man leaves. Then he comes back because he forgot his wallet and catches her. If three years of fights taught me anything, it's that he would never let me leave. It had to be this way.

In a frenzy, I tried to write a letter to leave with my engagement ring. My heart thumping, my hand shaking, my mind blank. I had no idea what I'd do for work, how I'd pay off my credit cards, how I'd get my car back. Then the baby starts crying. Shoot, what did we name her again? I can never remember.

"That's OK, my lil' bunny. Have some milk, and Mommy will figure this out."

And now I have to text Daddy, "I love you," for the fifth time today so he won't get suspicious.

The baby screamed every time I took bags to the car, and the guilt was almost crippling. We stopped at Target to get a car seat and hit the highway.

We got settled in Alexys' basement. I lay in bed nursing my daughter that night, and a profound sense of calm washed over me, followed by the growing certainty in my heart, assuring my soul I did the right thing. Even if I'm alone forever, that would be OK. Even if I live in this basement forever, that would be OK.

Over the next few years, I started making my way back to the woman I knew I was meant to be. The woman who exercises, who has a morning routine, good friends, and a fulfilling career. On January 1, 2020, I moved into the house I bought.

In 2022, I took my career into my own hands and started my own business.

Even now, the everyday things like late-night snacking in our underwear are special because I know there is a parallel universe where I stayed, and Mommy and Daddy were in another fight for God knows what.

What's most important is my daughter is confident, opinionated, and outgoing. She's learning Spanish at school and jujitsu in the afternoons. We play at the park, see the Reptile Man, and read before bed every night.

My daughter did not see her dad shove her mom to the floor, but she did see her mother buy a house, start a company, and travel. She sees men leave me flowers. She sees my amazing friends come together to celebrate our milestones and go on spa trips.

We all have the ability to give back to the world through our innate gifts and experiences. Many of us are taught to be selfless, to sacrifice our dreams for the sake of family or obligation when really, we have the duty to discover our highest selves.

I can guarantee I am a better resource to my loved ones as a happy woman, who is financially independent than if I were a miserable mom who stayed for the kids.

Let this story be a reminder that it's OK to ask for help.

And when someone shows you who they are, believe them.

Even though this chapter was excruciating, I am grateful for the resilience I have now. The lesson from this decade were to find my voice and not to roll over in the face of conflict.

When I was getting screamed at in the Madrid airport, I had no idea it was because I needed to learn to stand up for myself and find my voice. I've paid the ultimate price by not asserting myself. I lost my son because I couldn't find my voice. My daughter has that name because I couldn't find my voice. I gave my power away again and again and outsourced important decisions, like who I would marry!

I was so afraid of making the wrong decision, and I didn't have confidence in myself to run my own life. Now I know that there are no mistakes, only lessons. If I do make a choice that results in something difficult, I know I can handle it, I can course-correct, and I'm learning the lesson I need. I trust the unfolding of my life.

Now, when I'm faced with a difficult conversation, I know I must rise to meet the challenge, trusting the skills and instincts I've earned over the last decade. Every time I get over the discomfort and handle a conflict, it's an offering to the younger version of myself, to the version of myself who thought, "If I just don't do these things, he won't be mad, and we can be happy."

I recently spent a Friday afternoon with a man who drew me a bath with wine and candles. He shaved my legs and read to me before lotioning me and tucking me in bed. You better believe that's an offering to middle-school Sarah who never stood a chance with any of the cute boys; the Sarah who ate lunch alone

I can see her in my mind's eye, tattoo choker, slicked-back bun, and she'selated we grew into such a fierce woman.

ABOUT SARAH MAGILL

Sarah Magill is a serial entrepreneur, visionary coach, and magnetic speaker who specializes in turning dreams into plans and plans into unapologetic success. Sarah built massive resilience through abuse, child loss, financial desperation, and a complete loss of self. With much support from loved ones, she managed to run away, buy a home, start a business, and build a life she truly loves. She shows entrepreneurs how to share their stories and experiences authentically on social media and use these platforms to grow their businesses.

With a degree in Cultural Anthropology and Business Administration, and a lifetime of potent lived experiences, Sarah weaves a deep understanding of human connection with sharp business acumen to help visionaries own their spotlight.

Behind the bold moves is a woman who's traveled the globe, survived life's hardest moments, and emerged stronger. Her journey is a testament to self-mastery, courage, and feminine resilience. She's dedicated to living in full color and showing others how to do the same.

When she's not coaching or creating, you'll find her planning her next trip, dancing in the kitchen, and spending time with her bold and brilliant daughter.

Learn more about Sarah on social media

@_The_Reel_Sarah or at www.TheReelSarah.com

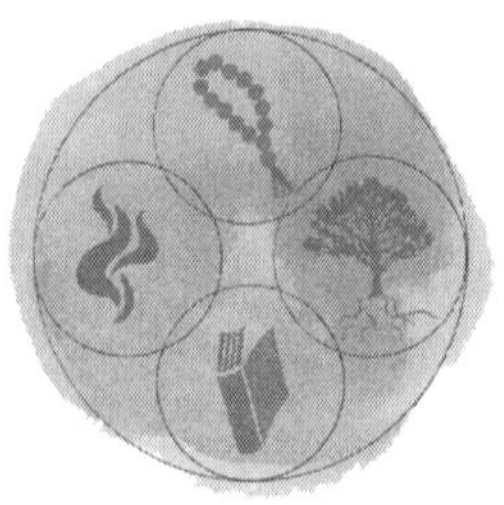

THERE IS A SOLUTION TO EVERY PROBLEM

Kathleen McCray

My story was tragic. And it is fascinating. It would be hard to believe it happened if I didn't know my story through experience.

My first recollection of consciousness was met with a feeling of uncertainty. Not only was I apprehensive about my everyday life, but I remember having a recurring nightmare for most of my childhood before adolescence. In this dream, I am standing at the top of steep stairs. These were the stairs that led up to my bedroom in the attic. In this dream, I jump from the top of the stairs, and while I am falling, I feel fear that jolts me awake before I reach the bottom.

As it turns out, unbeknownst to me in my early years, I was born into a functional alcoholic family with parents who were not equipped for the complex and demanding situations they were to face. While my mom and dad were setting up their lives as members of the silent generation (Do as you are expected to do), they did not learn the tools necessary to navigate the life they were generating.

My parents imparted many learning points that helped me

in my life's journey. I love them both very much. Perhaps they should have known to behave differently, but I can't judge that to be so. I am very grateful for the many things they did for me and our family. I think they did their best for what they had at the time and with the history that they experienced in their own lives. That said, their inabilities affected my life.

While I was molested on a few occasions by the adolescent son of my mom's best friend when I was approximately four years old and under his supervision, that was only the beginning of the emotional obstacles I would need to overcome in my life journey. The most significant theft of my character and spirit happened in my twelfth year. I started school one year later than my cohorts, so at twelve, I entered seventh grade and turned thirteen that November.

That year, my school hired a new music teacher. She was from a different city but relocated to my city to take a new position at my school. She was also given the responsibility of the choir director for the church.

At that time, my best friend and her mom were going to join the new choir. So, my friend suggested that my mom and I should join too. Since my mom loved to sing, she was delighted with the invitation, and she and I also joined.

I liked singing in the choir, and so did my mom. I don't remember exactly when I started feeling uncomfortable. The new teacher/choir director (I will call her Shelly) took a liking to my friend and me. I am not sure exactly what happened, but Shelly first began talking with my friend and me at choir practices. Then, at school she would invite us to visit her after we ate lunch and before we returned to class. She even stayed overnight with me and my friend at my friend's house. To this day, I am still not sure where the adults were. Eventually, Shelly made friends with my parents. This process took almost the entire first year she was employed at my school. After she secured my parents' trust, I was permitted to "hang out" with her at her apartment.

It is fitting to mention that I was a substantial disciplinary challenge for my parents before Shelly petitioned to be my friend. I was the actor in my family who said, "Alarm!!! Something is wrong here!!!" I started smoking tobacco and marijuana at eleven years old. I was caught stealing cigarettes with my friends. I would leave school without permission. My parents did not know what to do with me. They didn't understand themselves either. Their background and the myriads of problems from alcoholism in their life led them to deny any issue with our family. This was a family problem, but they could not face anything at that time.

So . . . my life was an uncomfortable shame for the next four years. My sister's boyfriend alarmed my mom and dad that he thought that Shelly was a pedophile. My mom asked me what I did when I was at Shelly's. I told her we listened to music and talked. After that, she never mentioned that topic again. I didn't either. I think she knew.

Shelly would tell me that I was homosexual when I didn't even know what that meant, and at the time, it sounded to me like it was something shameful. She also told me that I should date boys from school so that I would have that experience. I still don't understand her intent there, except maybe she wanted to dampen down her guilt about affecting my life so destructively. Later, I thought she might want a cover for the sexual relationship she imparted to me. Regardless of her motives, she changed my life forever.

When I turned eighteen, Shelly asked me to move in with her. I was still living at home with my parents. I told my sister about Shelly's invitation, and she warned me not to move in with Shelly because she was very controlling. My sister explained that I didn't yet know who I was, and I needed to better understand what I wanted for my future before I made a commitment to living with someone else. I took my sister's advice. I told Shelly I did not want to move in at the time. Shelly told me she had found another girlfriend. This time, the girlfriend was an adult.

The day I learned that Shelly had found a new girlfriend, I cried for an entire night. Yes, all night long. I was crushed that Shelly no longer wanted anything to do with me. The relationship was always abusive, but the victim doesn't understand that and grows accustomed to the relationship. What I didn't know was that was the best outcome for me. I am extremely grateful for the choice that Shelly made.

From here (as I now know), to escape, I decided to move to Colorado. In fact, I had reached the point in my life that I wanted to be left alone. I was twenty years old. Once living in Colorado, I found my way into a group of people that I thought I could trust. It turned out that these folks were also struggling with trauma from their past lives. They were isolating themselves from their families and society, teaching me to do the same. Having struggled with acceptance historically, I joined and marched to that call. While in this group, I met and married my husband. We were both products of abusive lives, and we were a comfort to each other. Until we were not. As I reflect on our life together, my husband and I both suffered from rejection as children. We also were accustomed to mental and, in some cases, physical abuse. It may be hard to believe, but to us, it all looked normal. In an effort to cope with extreme group-driven abuse (we started to question group leaders, and that didn't go well for our status within the group), we drank too much together as our choice of coping skills. Along with the stresses imposed by the group, my husband suffered ageism at work, and he became a very angry person. I also must interject that the group we belonged to for decades was no help because so many of them were also products of childhood abuse, and their trauma as children led to the same unhealthy relationships. We left the group.

Now, the recovery begins. About four years prior to this writing, I wrote in my journal that if my husband did not change his abusive behavior, I would leave. Two years after that journal entry, I left. The fifteen months that I lived alone, I studied every self-help book I could find. I employed a counselor to sort out how I got into all the problems in my life. While I was busy putting my life back together, my husband quit drinking, employed his own counselor, and sorted through how and why he designed his life in such a way.

Now the reason why I wanted to tell my story: It is because it doesn't end with just realization and recovery. The best part of my story is that at any point during the happenings of negative variables of my life, my story could have been different. For example, my parents could have been better equipped as parents. The teachers at my school could have intervened and taken Shelly out and away from children (she was fired, but they never told my parents why). Her professional demise was a direct result of her sexual abuse of me, but she never suffered any consequences. In fact, my mom even helped arrange a job for her with my mom's friend who was an executive at a large retail company. She stepped into her new job as a store manager, complete with a raise.

As long as I can remember, I wanted to help others out of situations that they may find themselves stuck in. Even before I understood what I was facing, I wanted to help anyone in need. I believe I wanted to help others because I knew I could help. One might say I felt a need to help because there was so much abuse around me from a very young child. Whatever the root cause for my interest in other people was, I now knew that I could help.

I am here to say that any problem a person, family, or organization has is absolutely fixable. I have spent decades studying abuse. As a child, I didn't have the cognitive ability to discern what was happening to me, let alone why it happened. From my childish point of view, my days were filled with have-to-dos, and don't ask why. Today, I understand what happened. Through my self-work, I know why it happened.

I want the reader to know that no matter how large a problem you suspect or how scary it would be to pull back the rug to look underneath, you ARE capable of looking. In those dark days when I wanted to run away, disappear, or drink poison to get someone else to stop what he or she was doing, I never once thought that there was any happiness, safety, or peace. Moreover, I never thought there was a solution. I was depressed and ashamed and hopeless.

There is absolutely a solution to every single problem. In my original career as an engineer, I complained to my boss that there sure were a lot of problems with the product that we were qualifying. He looked at me and said, "Be happy, Kathleen. If there weren't any problems, we wouldn't need engineers." The problems that we have in our lives are there because we need to solve them. I know now because I have evidence that provides proof that any jam you find yourself in, even if you cannot see a solution yourself, there is help available.

I am living a peaceful, safe, and exciting life now. My husband and I are different people than before we identified our wounds and healed our souls and spirits. We are excited every day, waking up together and jumping into the day's agenda. I cannot imagine having to live another single day as an injured person. We are happy to have worked alone and then together to reprogram our misinformed minds, which were programmed with someone else's flawed program. We are looking forward to our 30th wedding anniversary, which we will celebrate in March 2025!

ABOUT KATHLEEN MCCRAY

Kathleen is a retired engineer. She has a bachelor's in electrical engineering technology, an MBA, and a Master's in organizational leadership. Kathleen has been studying abuse and addiction for several decades. She is an author, trainer, and public speaker. Her latest book, *Diversity, Equity, and Inclusion in the Workplace*, is an introductory book on the DEI dilemma, with the aim of demystifying the DEI concepts.

Kathleen's experiences of abuse and recovery have led her to understand that there is indeed a solution to every problem. Kathleen can be reached at kathleen.mccray2020@gmail.com

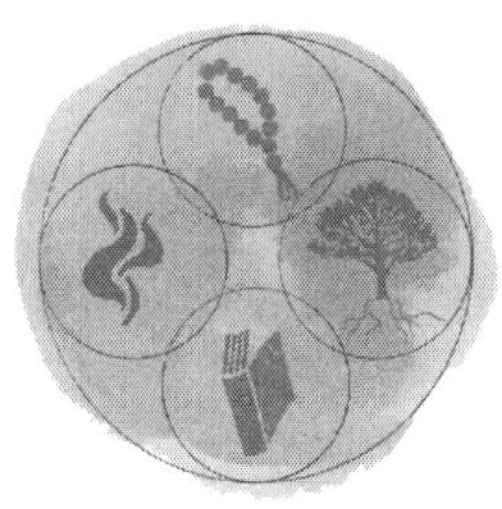

BELIEVE BEYOND THE BLUEPRINT: TRUSTING THE PROCESS OF INSPIRED ACTION

Sylvia Morrison

Living beyond belief is a life of trusting that the mastermind of this whole universe is supporting my journey and has my back. Beyond belief, I listen to my intuition and act on its messages. When I feel afraid, I acknowledge my fear and go inward to be in communion with the power that lives within me. I believe that life is always seeking to express its brilliance and creativity through each of us, so daily, I commit to live beyond believing in situations and circumstances. I remind myself that whatever is required to live the vision that I've been given will arrive in the same manner that the vision did.

My journey to Ghana began in December 2003. In conversation about Christmas shopping, my friend told me that instead of Christmas shopping, she was sending money to her mother in Ghana so that she could host a Christmas party for children in her village. It sounded like a noble idea, and I felt inspired to participate, so I offered to help. I gave my friend $75.00 to help fund the party. Two months later, my friend came to visit and brought me photos from the party. My heart was bursting with gratitude that I had helped to make it possible for these kids to have such an enjoyable time together. I asked many questions about the children, and then she told me that many of these kids were not attending school. That broke my heart, and I decided to do what I could to help. I asked for a list of the names of children and chose six names of children whose school fees I would pay.

After paying school fees for three years, I decided to visit Ghana in 2006. This was the beginning of my journey home to myself. For six years, I would travel to Ghana for a month or two, feeling a special connection to the people and place. It felt like I was living a dream from my childhood, but there was something missing. I missed seeing children with books in hand and reading. On my visits during those years, I would travel throughout Ghana and noticed that children did not have access to libraries and books. I felt called to do something about that.

I was born and raised in Jamaica. Like these Ghanaian children, my family did not have access to lots of money and other resources, but there was a little library in my village, very close to my home. Each afternoon, I would wait to see the librarian entering the library and immediately make my way there and stay there, reading until she was ready to go home. I loved reading, and I traveled the world through books. This caused me to expand my imagination, increased my sense of self, and gave me other perspectives of the world around me. Whenever I saw a book about Africa in the library, I would quickly borrow it and read it cover to cover. I had a strong belief deep inside me that I was an African child. I also dreamed that I would one day travel to Africa.

Although I was the only one of ten children in my family who made it to and graduated from college, it was no surprise to my parents that I chose teaching as my career path. I taught for 11 years in Jamaica before migrating to Canada, and after many years of exploration, I went back to the classroom. This time, teaching college students.

In the fall semester of 2012, I opened the door of my classroom at the college to welcome my class of first-year students. During the introductory activity, we took turns completing the statement, "If I had a million dollars, I would..." When it was my turn to respond, I mentioned that I would spend a portion of my million dollars building libraries in Ghana. A student inquired whether this was fantasy or real. Although I had not yet created the first library, I said it was real and then added that in the spring semester, some students would have the opportunity to participate in an international placement in Ghana.

As soon as those words fell from my mouth, a student raised her hand and blurted out a question, "Miss, I would love to go on that placement. How do I apply?" A shock wave went through my body, and my heart skipped a beat. I did not know what to tell her at that moment because I did not have the details. This idea was one that had been in my heart for many years.

I had been a member of a group of college students who participated in an international placement in Cuba. One of the community projects that we got to visit was run by an artist, Mr. Pelligrin. As he took us on the tour of the gallery and various workstations, explaining the programs and telling stories about the youth in these programs, I noticed myself feeling drawn in. I wanted to hear more. The tour ended, and we got back on our bus and returned to the place we were staying. There was a feeling of unrest inside me, so I asked permission to visit that community arts project and meet with Mr. Pelligrin during my "free time."

On this visit, I learned that the gallery was not only a gallery. It was Mr. Pelligrin's home. He was among the best artists in Cuba, and for many years, he thought about teaching art to youth in his community. He had unsuccessfully applied for government funding and tried various ways to finance his idea. After a few years, he could wait no longer, so he decided to use his house and entire yard for the project: an art center with various workstations and a gallery. Every room in his house was dedicated to the project. The only personal space was the smallest room, his bedroom.

I felt deep admiration for his service, his genuine care for the youth that he served, and his passionate commitment to using what he had to create positive change in his community. I left Cuba thinking about what I learned from Mr. Pelligrin, and I knew that I wanted to follow his example. I didn't know when, where, or how.

The dream that had been percolating in my heart for many years had now decided to announce its presence to the class before I was ready. I quickly told the student that we would have a conversation at the end of class that day. She approached me during our break, and I reminded her to see me at the end of class. I needed help from a higher power. I spent the ten-minute break in the washroom, asking the Spirit for the answer to her question so that I would be able to tell her about the application process at the end of class. The answer came. I was relieved when I told her that the first step of the process was to send me her resumé. I was sure that she would take days to prepare her resumé, and this would give me time to think through the details of the Ghana International Placement. I was wrong.

When I arrived at my office and checked emails later that day, I was shocked to see an email from her. I did not read it because I was not ready to reply. Within a week, there were ten resumés in my inbox from students applying to do their placement in Ghana. Over the next two months, I outlined the process, interviewed and selected students, invited interested community members to participate, and had a group of sixteen people preparing to travel with me to visit Ghana for the first time.

I did not have all the details when I made the announcement in my classroom that day in September 2012. In the months that followed until we arrived in Ghana in May 2013, I kept adding the next step as it became clear to me. We all landed in Ghana filled with excitement, joy, great anticipation, gratitude, and a sense of purpose. We were changing our lives in ways that we could not imagine or articulate. During our visit, we completed the first library and developed new relationships in a completely different country and culture. We learned and practiced new skills, gained new knowledge, and changed our worldview on many topics. We were inspired, attended to some of our traumas, and connected with parts of ourselves that were left dormant for too long. We created a legacy and transformed thousands of lives, including our own. Since then, Links Across Borders has created eight libraries and coordinated over 200 service abroad experiences in Ghana.

You do not need all the details before you make the move on the dream in your heart or the inspiring idea that has popped into your mind. Believe beyond your current knowledge, place, and experience. Believe that the pieces will come together and fall into place. I believe that our dreams are connected. The people and support that are needed are available and you will meet them on the way. They are waiting for you to show up. Start moving, taking one step after the other.

When my student asked me about the application process, I could have backed out because I didn't know what the process would be. When I saw ten resumés in my email inbox, I could have allowed the fear to stop me, but I didn't. I used fear to forge forward and create the process. I didn't know what it would take to organize a community and build a library. Activating this dream caused me to grow. I've become a more passionate teacher and speaker as a result of believing beyond what I know. Acting on my dream has connected me with the people that I'm here to help and the ones who are here to help me.

Your dream will cause you to grow.

After returning to Ghana annually for years and completing eight libraries, I began to notice a sense that something was missing. In my mind, I had the image of each library being a vibrant community space with children rushing in and out carrying books. We didn't have that because we needed resources: people, money to secure supplies, pay stipends, and secure reliable transportation. As I pondered about a solution for this challenge, the thought that came in very strongly was "Be on the ground." I was not ready for that and didn't know how that could happen anytime soon. For months, I contemplated and prayed about this idea.

I was on my way to the college on a very cold winter morning, and as I rushed across the street to get on the bus for my usual morning ride into the city, I heard a whisper, "Make this your last winter." This was an electrifying thought. The feeling traveled through every cell of my body, and I was transported to the place where my heart calls home: hot, sunny Ghana. For the entire ride into the city, I was on the ground in Ghana organizing a team, creating programs, exploring opportunities for collaboration. By the time I arrived at the college that day, I knew something had changed in me. The vision of being on the ground in Ghana was working on the idea of making each library a vibrant community space where children would be seen arriving and leaving with books.

When you receive an inspired idea, you have two choices. You can argue the idea away, or you can allow it to flow and fill you with whatever it brings. If you choose to argue it away, you will find good reasons why it cannot be done now and probably never. Most certainly never to be done by you. If you choose to allow the idea to flow, you could be filled completely with the delight of this vision, intoxicated with the transformation that there's no room for doubt or worry. It could cause you to grow and believe beyond your past conditioning that this can be done and that you are the one to do it.

This is when you will also notice that you are filled with ideas that support the vision. You will begin to meet people, your helpers, who are ready to collaborate. You will begin to learn new knowledge and skills, gain new insights, and stretch yourself in ways you hadn't imagined.

For months I lived with the question: "How will I make this happen?" Little by little, the answer arrived, and I took action, a step at a time. Within a year, I made the decision, sold my house, gave away most of my belongings, hosted a gratitude party with friends, loved ones, my community, and said goodbye because I decided to "Be on the ground" in Ghana. There were more questions than answers. I couldn't explain, but I knew that I was being called to go. By the end of 2019, I landed in Ghana with a container of supplies, some money in the bank, and a plan of action. I would create and train a team to facilitate programs in the libraries. I would travel for speaking and consulting to generate income, and we would create a leadership institute to mentor young adults in principles for life mastery. I felt completely prepared, proud of myself for making such a bold move, and delighted that I was finally home.

In January 2020, I said yes to an opportunity for a consulting project in Palestine. My trip was planned, airline tickets and hotel accommodations secured, and I was very happy that my well thought out plan of action was working.

When I began hearing news of the pandemic, my first reaction was gratitude that I was in a small village where COVID-19 could not find me, so I would not be affected. I prayed for my loved ones and others who were not as fortunate as I thought I was. The news continued to build, the world was forced into lockdown, and so was my plan of action for international travel, speaking, and consulting. I spent weeks contemplating the question, "What now?" Then, a bright idea presented itself. I could take the time to build the house that I had in mind, my home in Ghana. That was a great opportunity to use the time and focus on this project. I had the money, the design, and there were more than enough builders. I had never managed a construction project before, and I do not communicate in the local language.

How is this going to work? Yes, I will hire a contractor, but how will I express exactly what I want so that they build what I want instead of what they think?

We began the construction project, and within months, I knew I had to make a choice. I could accept that my moving to Ghana was a mistake and return to Canada, or I could make a commitment to face the challenges and be with the project to completion. This was the hardest thing that I have ever done. There were nights when I cried in bed and prayed that I wouldn't lose my mind. There were days when I thought I was going crazy. During this process, I experienced the worst and best in the local people. I grew in my commitment to the vision. I learned to trust my intuition. I grew in patience, compassion, and self-awareness. The forest became my friend, and I learned to be in communion with trees. My dream caused me to grow beyond belief.

Within two years, we completed construction, and I took occupancy of the house. I was so grateful to have my own yard and space to grow fruits and vegetables. Spending time in the yard, playing in the dirt, and planting seeds became one of my favorite things to do. I loved being greeted by the birds singing each morning. They soon became family members, coming to my window and hanging out on the verandah.

The world was still in lockdown, and some schools were beginning to resume classes, but this was an extremely difficult situation for parents, teachers, and students. The education system was very negatively affected by the lockdown. Most students and teachers, especially in rural communities, did not have access to computers, so they did not have lessons online, as was announced. The students were way behind in their curriculum and expected to be on par with their counterparts in cities and families who had access to the online space. I thought about how I could help. The gloom and doom in the news and everywhere was taking a toll on the teachers and students. I decided to do something that seemed illogical. I decided to launch the Links

Across Borders WeSHINE program. This program includes performing and visual arts, reading clubs, and the experience adventures library. Each of these required more money than Links Across Borders could provide. I had another decision to make. We had no idea for how long the rolling lockdowns would continue, neither did we know if/when the world could return to life as we knew it. Would I ever be able to proceed with my plan for income generation and funding?

I had my own house and yard space. I had some money in the bank, lots of learning supplies, and great health. I made the decision that I couldn't share with anyone. I just didn't want anyone to try to talk me out of it. I launched the programs one by one. I facilitated more reading clubs. We began taking students and teachers on excursions to nearby and faraway places. These excursions provided outdoor learning experiences that broadened their worldview, expanded their imagination, and increased their creativity and ability to express themselves. All this was quite costly, and we had no funding, but I decided that being in contribution was more important than having money in the bank. While my peers were protecting their "nest eggs," I was using mine to transform children's lives and becoming more of myself in Ghana. After three years, I had very little money left. This was the stark reality, and fear became my close companion.

I began to think seriously, with big fear and trembling, about money. How can I acquire money and wealth? I am a good person who is committed to doing good in the world, why am I not rich? Wallace Wattles's *The Science of Getting Rich* had been sitting on my bookshelf for years. Something told me it was time to read it and that started me on a path to a new mindset and relationship with money. I began to believe beyond my knowledge and skills that I could have the money to fund my vision if I did the internal work and created the environment to attract what I desired.

When you stretch beyond belief of what you know, beyond

your own limiting beliefs, and beyond beliefs in old paradigms, you will attract miracles and "Out of the Blue" events.

I made it my responsibility to focus on healing my money traumas. I invested money and time into learning about money. I hired mentors to guide me into finding my blocks and the deep-seated traumas that had me locked in a scarcity mindset. After a year of building new beliefs, paradigms, and a relationship with money, I began to release the belief that I had to be the one responsible for generating all the money needed to fund Links Across Borders and support children's education in Ghana.

I focused on the personal work of retraining my subconscious mind to believe that money is everywhere and that I will have more than I need by doing the inner work and being open to receiving. I decided that I would be gentle and compassionate with myself. I released the embarrassment and began to celebrate our accomplishments, give thanks for the wins, and focus on the good in everything. I began to share my new learning with others, including my new clients and community members. Each time that I shared with someone else, it strengthened my belief.

Soon, opportunities to receive or generate money came from unexpected sources, and I kept saying, "yes, thank you" while making adjustments along the way. I began to believe that there are many other people in the world who would support children's education in Ghana if I would let them know of this opportunity to do so. I reminded myself that our dreams are connected. I took on the responsibility of sharing about our programs and invited others to participate.

Out of the blue, I began to receive requests from individuals who wanted to experience Ghana with us. Guest Hosting is one of the ways that we generate money for our programs. Within a four-month period, we began to see evidence of financial support in ways that we did not anticipate. One company offered to fund the WeSHINE program for four years. A dream that Links Across Borders had for the I CAN Club was that they would write a story that would be published in 2024. I was blown away when we received full funding to write and publish *Life In A Ghanaian Village*. It became a #1 release and Amazon bestseller on launch day, October 8, 2024.

I truly agree and have evidence to prove that the circumstances of our lives are the curriculum for our evolution. Looking back at my life from this vantage point, I can see that each challenge on my journey that seemed like a setback was used to propel me forward. We have experienced the hardest years at Links Across Borders in the past four years and have had the most successes, initiated the most life-changing projects, and attracted more supporters than before.

My hope for you as you come the end of this chapter, is that you will remember that your dream will cause you to grow. The sensation that you're feeling that resembles fear is the force of your power to stretch and grow. Look beyond the current situation and connect with the source of your power. Believe that you are made for this, and all the supports that you need are available to you. Take the step in the direction of your dream. Give thanks always. Your sincere practice of gratitude will cause you to vibrate at the frequency that matches the vision you are holding and attract to you your desires. It is my hope that this chapter encourages you to ACT beyond old beliefs so that you can live the life of Fulfilment and Freedom that you desire and deserve.

Learn more about Links Across Borders at
https://linksacrossborders.org/

We would be delighted to hear from you.

ABOUT SYLVIA MORRISON

Author, Speaker, Humanitarian, And Coach, Sylvia Morrison Believes that "Everyone has what it takes to create the change that they desire by doing one small thing"

Sylvia is the Founder of Links Across Borders, a non-profit organization that co-creates

libraries, and facilitates educational programs for children in Ghana, West Africa.

In the best selling book; Inspired Living: A Guide to Ignite Joy and Prosperity, Sylvia Morrison shares her personal journey of creating the life she desires by taking inspired actions. She's the author of two best selling children's books. Grace's Lunch, and Life In A Ghanaian Village.

Ms. Morrison facilitates service abroad experiences in Ghana, transformational women's retreat, and a reliable Five Step Process that moves participants from feeling overwhelmed and stuck, to becoming clear, energized and activated, so that they can bring their unique gifts to the world.

Children's Book: https://tinyurl.com/GracesLunchUS
Websites: https://sylviamorrison.com/ https://linksacrossborders.org/
Instagram: https://www.instagram.com/iamsylviamorrison/
Facebook: https://web.facebook.com/sylvia.morrison.77

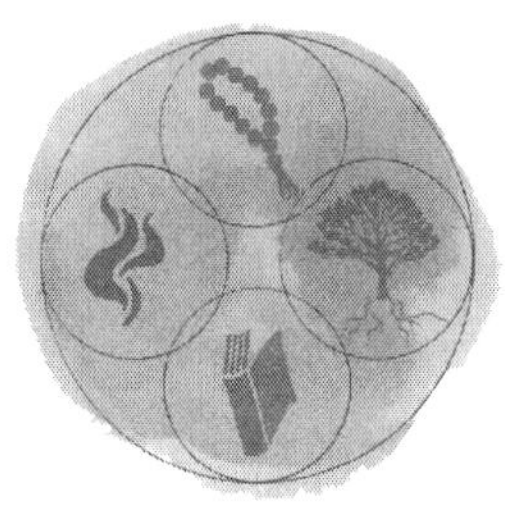

SENT TO ME

Kimberly Riddle

"Kim, honey, love," heavy breathing, rustling of the phone, and then silence was the last message that I received. I could tell by the desperation in his voice that something was wrong. I never thought that my return call to him would forever go unanswered.

For 30 years, my weekends were consumed with creating cakes for customers. I loved being a cake artist, but it often came at the expense of missing out on family activities and celebrations of our own. And our family vacations always revolved around my busy cake schedule. One day in February 2022, my husband walked into the kitchen while I was working on a cake, and I said, "What do you think about me taking this summer off?" He smiled from ear to ear. We discussed the impact that it would have on our finances while also acknowledging that our two youngest children would soon be at the age when it would be hard to get them to want to spend extended periods of time with us. And with that, we decided that I would take a June-September break from creating cakes. Months later, I would realize that even back then, the Universe was helping me by taking things off my plate, to relieve unneeded stress for what was coming up ahead.

In the month of May, I started to receive signs from my grandmother, who had passed away 12 years prior. It was smells that reminded me of her and subtle memories that would pop up out of nowhere. The end of June, my husband and I went on a long drive that took us close to the Brigham City cemetery where my family members are buried. I asked if we could stop for a visit. While I was in the store purchasing flowers, my husband entered the address into our GPS. I'm sure to avoid my back seat driving. As we drove through the cemetery gates, he stopped the truck and said, "Hun, look!" and pointed at the map. The directions were taking us to the EXACT location of where they are buried. "Your grandma must really want you to come visit." With tears in my eyes, I took a picture to capture that moment. At that time, these signs from my grandmother were merely just signs. They made me smile and warmed my heart. Although I did question why now after all of these years. And why me? Thirty days later, I would have my answer.

July 4th, "I really want to go to my Aunt Karen's house today and see my family." It had been years since I had last seen my extended family. Busy schedules and family conflict had kept us away in the past. But I knew in my heart that this was something that I needed to do. And so, we did. I will never forget the greetings that we received walking into her backyard. I could hear my grandmother say to me, "Kim, your posterity are your riches in this life." One of her many words of wisdom. Twenty-one days later, my Aunt Karen and her husband would jump in their car and drive hours away to be there for me during my greatest time of need.

Tuesday, July 19th. After six long months of my husband being home recovering from a shoulder injury, we were ready for him to hit the road. During his time off, he decided that he wanted to start his own transportation company. His first trip was taking him from Utah to Arizona, to California, back to Arizona, and a final delivery in Idaho before returning back home in Utah.

He was so excited to start his new adventure. Full of so many hopes and dreams for what this would mean for our family and our future.

The first half of the trip went as smooth as could be. He was thrilled that all of his time and attention to detail while preparing for this trip was paying off. Thursday morning, as he picked up his last load in Arizona, he took a picture of his truck and trailer to show me "how good it looked." He then made his way toward Las Vegas, Nevada. A few hours later, the first call came in. "Love, something is wrong with the truck. I'm going to need to stop somewhere." For the next few hours, my attempts to check in with him would go unanswered. Panic started to set in. Over the last seven years, my husband would self-medicate to try to control his extreme anxiety and OCD. My fear was that if he was having truck problems and deadlines that had to be met, this could cause him to spiral into an unhealthy situation. I needed him to answer his phone!

Early Friday morning at 3:28 a.m., I received a text with photos of his truck gauges and because I was passed out asleep from pure exhaustion, I missed what would be his final phone call to me. Later that morning I would be filing a missing person report in Utah, Nevada, and Arizona. "Do you happen to have a photo of his truck and license plate?" "YES, I DO! He just sent me one yesterday."

Saturday afternoon, little old me, a woman from Utah with less than 175 friends on Facebook, created a post pleading for the public to keep an eye out for my husband. Sunday morning at 8:18 a.m. I received this message: "Hello, my name is Bobbie. I saw the truck and trailer in question. Both were parked in an empty lot right next to my house when I woke up Friday morning. We left for a movie at 9:40 and both were there. When we returned home at 12:45, the truck was gone. They were parked at the corner of Fleet and Anderson off the Desert Springs exit in Arizona. Let me know if there is anything else I can do to help." I also started to receive photos and messages from others telling me that they could see his truck. I called the different police agencies and told my kids that we'd found Dad. Wearing the same clothes that I had slept in from the day before, not bothering to do my hair or makeup, I immediately jumped in the car. After all, I was simply driving to an unknown location, about five hours away, to pick up my husband and bring him home. Nothing else mattered!

Tuesday morning, July 26th, started out the same as the previous days. Early morning meeting with the officers in charge and the search and rescue team. But today was a little different; with the temperature dropping from the 100's to the high 90's, they felt like it was a good time to also use the K-9 dog teams. It had been too hot the previous days. Hours later, an officer approached, "Mrs. Riddle, why don't you take a seat?" were the only words that I needed to hear. My cries immediately filled the Arizona skies. This can't possibly be the way that our story ends! I won't let it! And I knew in an instant that my life was never going to be the same.

After 2 ½ days of searching, my husband was found less than 700 feet from his truck, down a steep and densely covered cliff. My first glimmer in that moment happened when talking to the medical examiner who came to care for my husband. When she first arrived, I asked where they would be taking him, and she gave me the name of a city that I was not familiar with. All I wanted to do was to take him home. Hours later, after his body was retrieved and ready for transport, I asked again. This time, the answer was different. "I am going to be taking him to Lake Havasu." With those words, I fell to my knees. My husband had a love for that area. For years, he had been trying to convince me to move there. We even had a trip planned for early that fall. So, I knew that there was nowhere else on this earth that he would rather be. And I thanked her for giving me such a precious gift. The next few weeks, I questioned why he was not found sooner. And then the answer came. That time frame was not for us to save his life; it was for me. It was time that I spent pouring my heart and soul out to my husband. Loving him unconditionally until the very end.

In the days following, my awareness was knowing that laughter in our darkest times was a gift. And then it moved to knowing with everything in me that my husband was with us. He was helping me with difficult conversations, helping me make the hard decisions, and he was holding me up when I couldn't stand on my own. I think that the most transformative realization was that there is indeed life after death and that love transcends the boundaries of space and time. And it was this new awareness that lit a fire in me to embark on a journey of self-discovery and complete awareness. And I became determined to live a life of purpose and meaning.

From the beginning of my journey with grief, I made the choice to look for and acknowledge all of the tender mercies and signs sent to me by my husband and the Universe. I record each situation in a journal. It is a way that I keep my husband present in my life. I am often asked, "How do you know it's a sign?" And my response is simple. It's your very first thought, it makes you smile, it makes you cry, it warms your heart. Never doubt your first instinct.

March 9, 2023, I woke to find that our power had gone out during the night. I told my son that we should get prepared for the next time. Minutes later, I had a knock on the door, and there was a package. I opened it to find a three-pack of flashlights. I didn't order flashlights. I called Costco; they didn't know how or why I had received them. The gentleman said, "Ma'am, the universe just really wanted you to have flashlights." To this day, I have not needed to use them. What I know now is that even back then, I was being told to let my light shine. Minutes later, I received an unexpected message from Kate Butler, whom I didn't know at the time, about an opportunity to attend Dare to Dream. It felt incredibly selfish of me to leave my family and also take finances away from our household. But I knew that this was a magical and potentially life-changing gift from the Universe. And it was. From that weekend, I learned that it is never too late to follow your heart, having a dream is God's way of pointing you in the right direction, and investing in yourself and your own happiness is a key part of living your best life. I was now craving anything and everything that felt good to my soul.

Shortly after riding this amazing high, my self-talk started to hold me back. I was constantly asking myself, "Why me?" I felt so unworthy of the magical journey that I was on. How could someone with so many skeletons in her closet really believe that an amazing life filled with so much potential was really possible? I struggled with this thought pattern for quite some time. And then, one day, over the period of 24 hours, the Universe made it crystal clear to me that before I moved any further, I needed to learn how to love me. And I dove in headfirst, and it was HARD! What I learned along the way was that these skeletons in my closet were not skeletons at all. They were actually stepping stones in my life that have made me the person that I am today. They have made me strong, taught me how to care and be understanding. They taught me how to be empathetic and how to love unconditionally. It's how I am able to relate to so many of the people I meet. I became grateful for this life that I have lived. And when I could finally look in the mirror and say, "Kim, I love you," the Universe was quick to respond with, "Now is the time to let your light shine." I was reminded of my desire to live a life of purpose and intention. I was reminded of how blessed I have been on my journey with grief.

Early in my grief, I was connected with a group of beautiful women who were also on the same journey. We quickly formed a bond like nothing I had ever felt before. To be able to find people who truly understand the depths of your sorrow without needing to say a word and yet also understand the meaning behind a smile or a laugh is priceless. But to bond with a group who also shared the same desire to live their best life has been an irreplaceable gift from God. The ladies would often say, "Kim, you need to start a group." The Universe also said, "Kim, you need to start a group." And in response to this calling, AWARE was formed. My acronym for AWARE is Acceptance of loss. Wounds of the heart. Angels around us. Remembrance cherished. Encouragement to live your best life. I knew that I wanted to use the infinity symbol as the logo, and without skipping a beat, my husband sent me a sign. I was sitting at my desk at work fiddling with some design ideas, and my mother-in-law walked in the door holding a bag, and she said, "I was just out shopping, and Beau said buy this for Kim, so I did." I opened the bag and found a large colored swirled glass infinity symbol. Oh, my beating heart!!

The vision behind this group is based upon my knowledge and experience that it takes an army to live this life. I wanted a place where people can meet and know that someone is listening, they are supported, and they have a team of people cheering them on. Celebrating each and every win, and a shoulder to cry on when things are hard. We are survivors empowered by the infinite capacity that our hearts have to heal. We believe that our loved ones are still with us and in the magic of the Universe. Being aware is believing that anything is possible. It's the way that we connect with ourselves, others, and the Universe. And it's having the courage that when the Universe opens a door, you walk through it.

To my husband,

Because of you, I am loved, beautiful, strong, confident, aware, enough, valued, and joyous. I am grateful!!

ABOUT KIMBERLY RIDDLE

Kimberly Riddle, proud mother of 6 children and grandmother of 12, never envisioned a life beyond the ordinary. Everything changed on July 26, 2022, when her husband left this earth. In the depth of her grief, grief became her teacher. Taking her on a journey of unexpected growth and self-discovery and showing her the quiet magic of the Universe. From this journey emerged AWARE. A grief support group she founded to help others navigate their grief and discover hope beyond the loss.

Inspired by the healing power of connection and helping others, she is also working on transforming her current business into The Chocolate Dealer. On a mission to uplift others, create community, and spread moments of sweetness in a world that sometimes feels bitter. In grief, in healing, and in life, we all need reminders that connection, comfort, and joy are always within reach.

You can connect with Kimberly Riddle at:

Awareness333@outlook.com
Facebook: @AWAREsupport
Facebook and Instagram: Kimberly Fluhrer Riddle
Sales@thechocolatedealer.store to get connected with amazing chocolatiers around the U.S. and to receive a discount code for an online purchase to make sweets of your own.

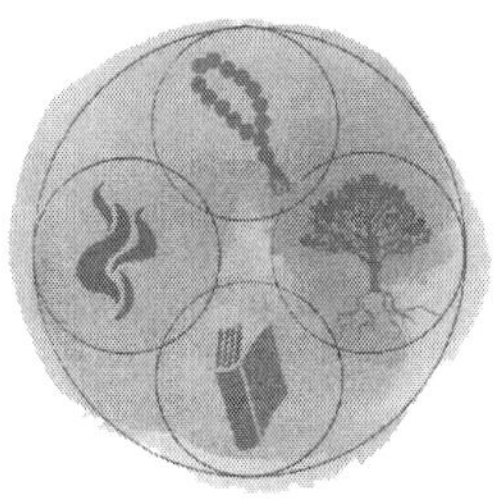

Have you ever dreamed of
becoming a published author?
Do you have a story to share?
Would the world benefit
from hearing your message?

Then we want to connect with you!

The *Inspired Impact Book Series* is looking to connect with women who desire to share their stories with the goal of inspiring others.

We want to hear your story!

Visit www.katebutlerbooks.com to learn more about becoming a Featured Author in the #1 International Best-selling *Inspired Impact Book Series*.

Everyone has a story to share!
Is it your time to create your legacy?

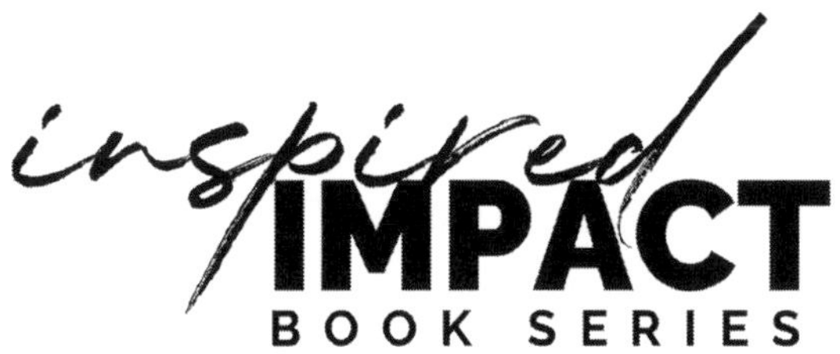

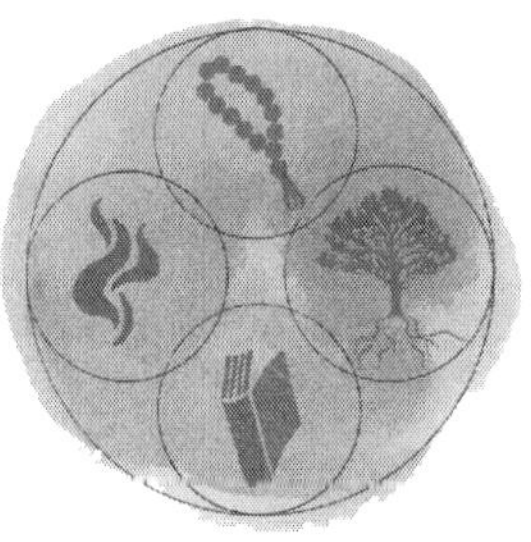

May your soul be uplifted and the words of these pages inspire you to continue to lead with your infinite divine light to your fullest expression in leaving your legacy!

Authors of Believe Beyond

REPRINTED WITH PERMISSIONS

Kate Butler, CPSC
Patty Aubery
Raida Abdulsalam Abu-Issa
Dr. Lucette Beall
Jenness Keller
Viktoriya Legkun
Barbara Lanz
Erin McCahill
Ericha Scott
Candice Shepard
Jessica Skop
Karen Smith
MiShawn Williams
Christina Giannone
Andrea Gutmann
Kelly Kinney
Nora Rose Mogielski
Tiffany Star
Anne Tyler
Eleni Yiambilis
Shanea Clancy
Sarah Magill
Kathleen McCray
Sylvia Morrison
Kimberly Riddle

Made in the USA
Middletown, DE
25 February 2025

71835031R00129